The Skills of Teaching:
Interpersonal Skills

Robert R. Carkhuff, Ph.D.

David H. Berenson, Ph.D.

Richard M. Pierce, Ph.D.

CARKHUFF
INSTITUTE
of HUMAN
TECHNOLOGY

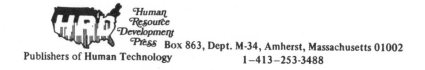

Human Resource Development Press

Box 863, Dept. M-34, Amherst, Massachusetts 01002

Publishers of Human Technology

1–413–253-3488

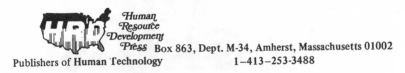

Human Resource Development Press

Publishers of **Human** Technology

Box 863, Dept. M-34, Amherst, Massachusetts 01002

1–413–253-3488

International Standard Book Number: 0-914234-20-X

Library of Congress Number: 74-75374

First Printing–January, 1977

Second Printing — March 1977

Designed and Illustrated by Tom Capolongo
Consulting Editors, Sally R. Berenson and David V. Rowland
Typography by Fran Morrier
Consulting Art Director, Eileen Donovan

10, 15

The Skills of Teaching:
Interpersonal Skills

TABLE
OF
CONTENTS

continued on next page

ABOUT THE AUTHORS

Dr. Robert R. Carkhuff (on the ladder) is Chairman, Carkhuff Institute of Human Technology. He has devoted his life to research and teaching. The author of more than two dozen books on helping and teaching effectiveness, Dr. Carkhuff is internationally renowned as the most-cited reference in the last decade in counseling psychology. A teacher at primary, secondary and post-secondary levels, he continues to coach youth baseball, basketball and football. Dr. Carkhuff is the developer of the human and educational resources development models upon which **The Skills of Teaching** series is based.

Dr. David H. Berenson (next to the waterwheel) is Director of Educational Technology, Carkhuff Institute of Human Technology. He specializes in teacher training and educational administration. Teaching for more than 15 years at primary and secondary grade levels, Dr. Berenson has spent the last 10 years revolutionizing pre-service and in-service teacher training programs. He has conducted pathfinding research in the development of effective educational delivery systems. Dr. Berenson is co-author of the entire **Skills of Teaching** series.

Dr. Richard M. Pierce (in the foreground) is Director of Human Technology, Carkhuff Institute of Human Technology. His specialty is conducting in-service teacher and counselor training programs. Dr. Pierce is an experienced counselor, having conducted college counseling center operations as well as family treatment centers specializing in parenting skills and learning-to-learn programs. Dr. Pierce is noted for his extensive research on the training of teachers and counselors. He is the co-author of **Helping Begins at Home** and **Teacher as Person.**

The Authors and Their Teachers

FOREWORD

Truly, the United States of America is one of the most remarkable countries in the world. Never before has any civilized country attempted to provide educational equity for all of its citizenry. The fact that we are moving from compulsory attendance (schooling) to education is exciting. Only a growing democracy could tolerate the ambiguity of so many critics and continue to move toward the common goal of education for all.

Within the universe of American education there is human life on at least two separate spheres. Neither of these spheres can be mathematically studied with the usual tools of geometry because they are not symmetrical or harmonious. Yet, both spheres rotate and revolve in the universe of education. Each has a dissimilar orbit—one moving from East to West, the other West to East. Both also travel at rapid rates, but are not certain where they are going.

Sphere #1 is composed of a somewhat artificial environment. It abounds with a variety of human species, some of whom have been classified as psychologists, philosophists, economists, sociologists, anthropologists, humanists and futurists. They also have two broad categories commonly named hard sciences and soft sciences. On occasion art erupts, but since it cannot be measured it lacks a registered classification. The "ists" rule.

Several strange life forms have evolved on Sphere #1. One form produces teachers who produce teachers to produce teachers. Many of these teachers never acquire the necessary skills of living, learning or working (career). Much of their time is devoted to the development of new words. These new words may be understood by a select few only. Also, these teachers reside in "higher education" institutions that are named colleges and universities. Often these teachers do not deal with learners in "lower education."

Sphere #2 has a real environment. It too has many varieties of human species. Three of these species are classified as children, parents and teachers. Each has something in common with the other—education. Parents have children. Children go to schools to be educated by teachers. Sometimes teachers and parents work together with the children to help them get an education. They do not always agree on what the content for learning is to be, but they know that children need skills in living, learning and working.

Sphere #2 receives confusing messages from Sphere #1 about education and the processes of learning. Many of these messages are sent by the "ists" who have not learned that individuals, if they are to be free, must understand the relationships of independence, dependence and interdependence. The "ists"

i

provide television for the children on Sphere #2. Unfortunately, a large number of children spend more time watching television than they do going to school. Most of the programs on television do not teach any skills to the children. Some observers of children note that the average child spends about 1000 hours in school and about 1500 hours watching television each year.

Arguments are characteristic of Sphere #2. Little agreement exists in what to do with children. Some of the "ists" urge the teachers and parents to have open classrooms; other "ists" want a return to the basic skills. Depending on their mood, Sphere #2 swings like the pendulum of a large clock to mixed messages. It can no longer keep accurate time.

Meanwhile, the overall achievement of the children is dropping. Confusion reigns. A few teachers and "ists" get together and begin to study the problem. Soon they discover that the problem is not children, but rather their own inability to carefully plan the skills needed for living, learning and working. They decide to build a human technology of skills for teaching. In the forefront of the effort to build a human technology are the authors of **The Skills of Teaching Series**. With more than a decade of research into teaching and helping processes and outcomes, Dr. Carkhuff and his colleagues have developed the necessary skills teaching programs for a human technology

for human effectiveness—skills teaching programs that will enable the children and parents as well as teachers to achieve and enjoy success.

At first the job is painful because they must examine their own behavior. What to organize first? The representatives of both spheres agree that teachers must have the teaching skills that they need to relate the learners to their learning experiences:

1. **interpersonal skills** which enable the teachers to enter the learners' frames of reference and prepare them for learning;
2. **content development skills** which enable the teachers to develop their specialty content to a skills objective;
3. **teaching delivery skills** which enable the teachers to deliver their specialty skills to the learners;
4. **learning strategies** which enable the teachers to involve their learners in exploring, understanding and acting upon their learning experiences; and
5. **learning transfer strategies** which enable the teachers to teach their learners to transfer their learnings to real-life applications.

Good teachers have known for years that teaching skills are the basis for learning. They have learned the joy of hard work and discipline as they taught their children. They notice that children are interested in learning because the teachers care about them and have the teaching skills to implement their care.

The Skills of Teaching represents a landmark in educational technology. These skills teaching programs were developed by and in conjunction with classroom teachers—those in the front lines of education. **The Skills of Teaching** teaches the kind of concrete skills a veteran teacher wishes s/he had when she began her teaching career. It's the kind of teacher training curriculum that an outstanding teacher-educator might develop over several decades.

There is no magic in teaching and learning. It is hard work. The "ists" from Sphere #1 come to Sphere #2 and join the real world. Freedom is too priceless to lose for lack of skills. Our human resources are too scarce to be wasted in fragmented ego trips. Human technology is being developed for and by humans. **The Skills of Teaching** enable teachers to master the teaching skills and at the same time begin to measure the progress of their learners. In time the learners are able to measure their individual progress and help to control the learning process.

With careful study and planning, teachers and parents soon discover that they are the source of their children's effectiveness. The outcomes are symmetry and harmony. One sphere emerges. It is called Earth. And the people on it are truly human beings. Because they recognize that all of their children are exceptional.

January, 1977   James W. Becker, Ed.D.
Washington, D.C. Executive Director,
        National Foundation
        for the
        Improvement of
        Education

FOREWORD

Do you wish to improve your **control** in the classroom?

Reduce **student absenteeism and tardiness?**

Reduce **student discipline and school crises?**

Do you wish to improve your teaching effectiveness in the classroom?

Accelerate **student learning skills?**

Accelerate **student cognitive growth?**

We did! And we found the teachers' levels of teaching skills to be significantly related to these learner outcomes!

How did we do it? By first learning and then teaching our teachers **The Skills of Teaching.** In the **National Consortium for Humanizing Education** we taught **The Skills of Teaching** to hundreds of elementary and secondary teachers all over the country. We studied the effects of our teacher training upon over 6,000 students.

What we found was that the learners of teachers with the skills of teaching demonstrated significantly greater growth and development. Most important, teachers could be systematically trained to develop their teaching skills.

Trained teachers were most effective in maintaining **control** and reducing **discipline** problems in the classroom. They were most effective in facilitating student achievement in the **basic skills.**

What did we learn from **The Skills of Teaching?** We learned the principles of learning and the teaching skills we needed to help our students to learn. The principles are gleaned from long (15 years) and exhaustive (hundreds of projects reviewed in more than two dozen books and hundreds of articles) by the most-cited author in counseling psychology, Dr. Robert R. Carkhuff, and his colleagues, life-long educator Dr. David H. Berenson and teacher-training specialist Dr. Richard M. Pierce. The principles of teaching as developed by the Carkhuff model are simple.

All learning begins with the learner's frame of reference. We teachers need interpersonal skills to enter the learner's frame of reference.

All learning culminates in a skills objective. We teachers need content development skills to develop our content to a skills objective.

All learning is delivered in atomistic steps. We teachers need teaching delivery skills to organize, stimulate, reinforce and manage learning.

All learning involves the learner in naturalistic learning processes. We teachers need the learning strategies to involve the learners in experiential exploration, personalized understanding and behavioral action.

All learning is transferable. We teachers need the teaching transfer skills to insure everyday living, learning and working applications.

All of these skills are captured in **The Skills of Teaching** series. Together, they constitute **the most revolutionary step forward in the history of education**. They define the skills in terms that are observable and measurable. In this respect, the skills are useable and repeatable. Because of this they are, for us as teachers, achievable. In brief, we teachers can learn these teaching skills and use them with our students. We can achieve positive student outcomes.

In attendance!

In discipline and citizenship!

In cognitive growth and achievement!

Indeed—in intelligence!

More than anything else, what teachers want are the teaching skills which insure their roles and discharge their function in American education.

Together, **The Skills of Teaching** constitute the teacher's answer to accountability: **to preserve the integrity of teaching and produce the accountability of outcome through expanding the quantity and quality of teaching skills.**

The Skills of Teaching picks up teaching skills with its principles, objectives and programs where others leave off with facts and concepts.

We owe a great debt of gratitude to Drs. Carkhuff, Berenson, Pierce and their associates for making possible the second greatest privilege in the world—teaching.

January, 1977   David N. Aspy, Ed.D.
Washington, D.C.   Executive Director,
                   National Consortium
                   for
                   Humanizing Education

PREFACE

This book is dedicated to the devoted teachers—forgotten yet burdened with the greatest responsibilities in the history of humankind. It is to these teachers that we offer a distillation of our efforts in nearly two decades of research into the effective ingredients of learning.

Our research program was a simple one. We studied in depth the dimensions of teachers who made a difference in the lives of their learners. We defined the teaching dimensions we found in observable and measurable terms. We then taught these dimensions to other similarly committed teachers in pre-service and in-service settings. The findings were exciting: in relatively brief periods of time, the teachers could learn the teaching skills which they needed to demonstrate a significant impact upon their learners. This impact was far greater than the impact of teachers who did not have these skills.

The teaching skills are not unknown to teachers. They include the **interpersonal skills** which enable the teacher to enter the learner's frame of reference. They emphasize the **content development skills** which allow the teacher to develop the content to a skills objective. They also emphasize the **teaching delivery skills** which enable the teacher to make the delivery of the skills to the learners. They incorporate the **learning strategies** which enable the teacher to involve the learner in learning. They culminate in the **learning transfer skills** which help the learner to use the skills in everyday life activities.

We found that, while these skills are known to teachers, the teachers have not always been taught them in ways that are observable and measurable, teachable and repeatable. We have refined these ways and offer them to you—as teachers to teachers—in the interest of our children and yours for generations to come.

In doing so, we wish to acknowledge the people who have been teachers to us.

Dr. David N. Aspy — *Executive Director, National Consortium for Humanizing Education,* who helped us develop . and teach our teaching skills to teachers in a national study of learning effectiveness.

Dr. James W. Becker — *Executive Director, National Foundation for the Improvement of Education,* who gave us an international and historical perspective of the teaching and learning systems within which teachers operate.

Sally R. Berenson — *Associate Director of Educational Technology, Carkhuff Institute of Human Technology,* who taught us how to teach teachers.

Dr. Bernard G. Berenson — *Director, Carkhuff Institute of Human Technology, who* has been our guiding mentor in the development of a human technology.

Dr. Andrew H. Griffin *Instructional and Professional Development Specialist, Liason with NCATE and AACTE, National Education Association,* who taught us the multicultural dimensions of interpersonal skills development.

Dr. Margaret "Peg" Jones *Associate Director, National Foundation for the Improvement of Education,* who guided us to a most profound understanding of the implications of entering the learners' frames of reference.

Dr. Shirley McCune *Director of Title IX Project, Chief State School Officers,* who taught us the dimensions of sexist curricular and systems and the critical implications for the development of all human beings.

Dr. Flora Roebuck *Director of Medical Education, Johns Hopkins University,* who helped us to operationalize teaching skills and analyze learning effects.

Hundreds of teachers—everywhere—who taught us how to teach. Thousands of learners —everywhere—who learned as we learned. As learners, we are eternally grateful for the teachings we have received. They made a difference in our lives. We hope—through these materials and accompanying teaching—we will make even a fraction of such a difference in your lives and your work. So that you, in turn, can do so for your children—your learners.

In this volume of **The Skills of Teaching,** we focus upon the teaching skills that help to get the learners ready for learning. Here we focus upon the teaching skills that help to prepare the learners to achieve their learning goals. These teaching skills emphasize the interpersonal dimensions of teaching.

Giving attention to the learners in order to involve the learner in learning.

Responding to the learners' frames of reference in order to help the learners explore their learning tasks.

Understanding the learners in order to help the learners set learning goals.

Initiating with the learners in order to help the learners achieve their learning goals.

These interpersonal skills will be the basic building blocks upon which you can build your own living, learning and working effectiveness as well as that of the learners whom you serve.

Amherst, Massachusetts   *R.R.C.*

January, 1977   *D.H.B.*

     R.M.P.

THE GOLD STAR SCHEDULE

Johnny was a bright little chap. Somehow through his home experience he had managed to develop and maintain his vast resources with some great degree of autonomy. Johnny. was physically strong; in his innocence he could feel all the feelings of the world, but his strongest resource of all was his intellect. Johnny could interpret and integrate experiences with the clarity and meaning which few adults could fathom.

But Johnny's independence sometimes got him into trouble, especially in school. Whereas the other first graders would color rows on rows of green leaves, he would color one or two leaves and draw a horizontal green arrow through the remaining leaves indicating the direction of the rows of leaves. The teacher always marked the paper "Careless" and made him do it over again. But in their next practice exercise, coloring columns of orange leaves, he would color one or two and draw his vertical orange arrow. And sometimes, to the teacher's dismay, he sat sideways in his chair while the other students sat facing the front as they were told. And even worse, sometimes he got up to get a drink without permission. The teacher was very distressed. Johnny's mother was very dismayed.

One day while the class was doing arithmetic problems, Johnny was busily drawing pictures.

"Johnny's not doing arithmetic!" a voice blurted out.

And the teacher stormed down the aisle.

"Johnny, you have been a most difficult pupil. You will sit in the corner for the rest of the day. And we will discuss your problem after school today."

And Johnny sat in the corner all day, drawing the rest of his pictures in his mind, so that at the end of the school day, the teacher had great difficulty in interrupting him to tell him that now he must stay after school.

Alone with Johnny, the teacher grimaced. *"He is the most difficult pupil I have ever had!"* she thought.

But she asked instead, *"What is it you were doing during our arithmetic session?"*

And Johnny answered with great excitement about his trip to the museum and Brontosauruses and Stegasauruses and Tyrannosauruses.

Johnny was doing a book on dinosaurs, his own idea, his own book.

"Let me see your pictures," the teacher requested.

With great glee, Johnny hurtled the rows of seats and brought his pictures to her.

The teacher flipped the pages, seeing the different kinds of dinosaurs that could come from eggs, seeing what the different dinosaurs ate and how they acquired their food. And finally, how the last of the great dinosaurs died off when mountains of ice covered their land.

The teacher looked at Johnny and pondered him.

"This is an interesting piece of work," she told him.

"I shall give you a gold star for it."

"You may go home now, Johnny."

"Thank you, teacher."

Johnny spent a lot of time reworking his dinosaur book, only he didn't do it during arithmetic any more. And he thought as he was reworking it, *"And I will get another gold star for this."*

Johnny sat down at his desk one day and thought, *"Gee, I'd like to get another gold star."* And he thought about how he could do this. And he thought that Mrs. Lester sure didn't like boys fighting. Maybe, he thought, he could take the pictures of the dinosaurs who were fighting out of his book.

"Those old carnivorous dinosaurs weren't necessary anyway. And maybe I can include some of the smaller, grass-eating dinosaurs. Mrs. Lester sure would like that!"

And he took his completed work to Mrs. Lester, happily pointing out the absence of the pictures of the Tyrannosaurus and the other nasty dinosaurs and the presence of some new, very small and mild-mannered dinosaurs for which he had a great deal of difficulty finding pictures to copy.

"This is an excellent book on dinosaurs." And Mrs. Lester gave Johnny another gold star, adding *"Now I want you to go to your seat and color the rows of red leaves, for you know, Johnny, it is the height of the Fall season."*

And Johnny went dutifully to his seat and colored rows and rows of red leaves.

In fact, Johnny is the best colorer of leaves in the class.

And the teacher never writes "Careless" on his paper anymore.

The teacher is very pleased with Johnny's progress.

Johnny's mother is very pleased with Johnny's progress.

EPILOGUE

One day Johnny looked up from his arithmetic lesson and saw that his friend, Jenny, was not doing the lesson. Why, Jenny was drawing something! Remembering how awful it felt when he was caught not doing his lesson, Johnny wanted to tell Jenny what was right. But he knew that no talking was allowed. Remembering that awful feeling, he raised his hand and asked for permission to approach the teacher's desk and talk personally to her. And he did. And no one in the class heard what he said to Mrs. Lester.

The Skills of Teaching:
Interpersonal Skills

INTRODUCTION

**YOU WILL NEVER FORGET
THE FIRST DAY OF SCHOOL**

   You will never forget! A long-ago learner, you walked into a classroom, quickly looked around, studied the teacher and decided. Was everything you heard from last year's kids true? Right then and there on the first day, you pretty much made up your mind about what kind of school year it would be. What were you looking at? What were you searching for? How did you know?

NOW YOU ARE THE TEACHER

You were so excited, wondering what it would be like. "What is this year going to be like? What's my teacher going to be like? Nice, I hope!"

Even now, 20 or more first-days-of-school later, you still have those feelings. It's always a little hard to fall asleep the night before the first day of school. You feel the butterflies fluttering around inside of you. You wonder what this school year is going to be like. Now maybe it will be different—now that **you** are the teacher!

YOU ARE PREPARED FOR SCHOOL

Anxiously, you make your last-minute preparations for the first school day. You check the bulletin board because you want your learners to see that you are organized. You review your lesson plan because you want your learners to know you are prepared. In front of the mirror, you make last-minute alterations in your appearance. You want your learners to see you as an attractive person because then they will want to be like you. This will make teaching a lot easier.

YOU WILL KNOW EACH LEARNER

Eagerly, you check over the class roster again for signs of comfort. Some of the names you recognize. You had their older brothers or sisters. You know their parents. You think about them for a moment. "What will they be like?" "What will the new ones be like?"

The moment they enter class, you will know them. You will know the quick learners as well as those who will have difficulty. What will you be looking at? What will you be looking for? How will you know?

YOU WILL USE ALL OF YOUR SENSES

As the learners crowd in, they become alive and real for you. Soon you will attach names to faces and products: Jimmy, the skinny little boy with haystack hair; Amanda, the girl whose assignments look as though she brought them to school in a lunchbox.... You use all of your senses to learn as much as you can. As they parade right in front of you, you can see and hear your learners' past experiences—at home and in school. Some children had good learning experiences and they are exciting to be with. Some had poor learning experiences and these children are sad!

YOU WILL EXPERIENCE
THE LEARNER FULLY

How do you know these things? You think for a moment. You can see the vitality of your learners in their energy and activity levels, their postures, their strides, everything about them. Harry's got his head down again; maybe not getting enough sleep.. Selby's small smile shouts as loudly as a more demonstrative child's laughter; she really worked for that 'A'.... You can hear their resourcefulness in their ranging responses, carefully integrated to meet the needs of each unique situation. You can experience the humanity of the persons within the fullness of their attention and the intensity of their interactions with others. Sure, there are other signs and sounds of life, sometimes mischievously outside the bounds of school propriety. Nevertheless, these are still lifeful evidence of the learners' potential to grow. Yes, there are, indeed, ways that you know who they are.

THE LEARNER WILL EXPERIENCE YOU FULLY

Then, how do they know you? You ponder this question. Perhaps in the same manner?! Yes, they know you in the same way that you know them! You become real and living for them when you greet them at the door. They will attach a name to your face and they will come to know you intimately by your products. For they will be your products!

HAVE YOU DONE ALL YOU CAN?

Yes, they will read you in the same way that you have read them. Perhaps not as well as if they were accomplished practitioners in the skill. But then again, perhaps quite well through the unfiltered experience of the naive and the innocent. For even the youngest child can recognize human warmth, attentiveness, concern—or the remote neutrality, the *"I'm busy, go away"* attitude which so many adults reveal in their words and behaviors. Yes, they will see your vitality—hear your resourcefulness—experience your humanity. And they will judge you much as you have judged them. You have done all that you can to prepare yourself for this moment. Or have you?

YOU MUST KNOW SOMETHING

Through the learners' eyes, you will also know who you are. For them or with them, you must ask and answer the basic questions about their teachers? *"Do they know something I don't know? Do they have something I want to have?"* With these fundamental questions, the learners define the goals of learning: *"Can the teacher help us to grow big?" "Can the teacher help us to get ourselves 'together?'"* Translated for teachers, this means, *"Can the teacher help us to grow physically, emotionally, socially and intellectually?"* If you can answer the question positively, then you have developed a basic ingredient of learning; you have motivated the learners to learn by demonstrating that you know something useful for them, that you can help them to learn.

YOU MUST HELP
THE LEARNER TO GROW

A wise person once said that you cannot flunk a child for a year's growth. When you think about it, you realize the truth of this statement. Whether we help them or not, the students are going to grow. They are going to grow physically in inches, pounds and muscle. They are going to grow emotionally in friendships and love relationships. They are going to grow intellectually in learning facts and developing concepts. The real challenge in teaching is what you have to offer your learners to help them fully. You have yourself as the model for their growth. You also have yourself as the agent for their growth.

YOU MUST HAVE SKILLS

It is simply not enough to have something to offer the learners to grow. There are many people who have skills in physical, emotional, social or intellectual areas who are unable to transmit them to others. Learners simply do not absorb learning by osmosis. Rather, there are real skills that you must have in order to help someone to grow. These skills are what separate professional teachers from other people.

YOU MUST HAVE INTERPERSONAL SKILLS

There are many sets of skills that you must have to be an effective teacher. First, you must have the interpersonal skills that enable you to develop the learning relationship. Interpersonal skills emphasize your communication skills. All teaching that you do is done in the context of an interpersonal relationship. Whatever you do, you are continuously influenced by the interpersonal input and shaped by the interpersonal feedback from your learners. Without skills, you can never discover the unique individuality of your Jimmys, Amandas, Harrys, Selbys; and without skills, you can never reach out to them as individuals and really touch their lives. Only skills allow communication. Yes, the teacher is a communicator. You must conquer the interpersonal skills necessary to communicate to your learners. Interpersonal skills are really the first set of teaching skills.

YOU MUST HAVE TEACHING SKILLS

There are many other teaching skills. In the context of a facilitative interpersonal relationship, you employ all of your teaching skills to achieve your educational objectives. You must conquer the skills involved in your educational specialty subject. You must be equipped with the skills involved in developing what and who and how you are going to teach. You must conquer the teaching skills necessary to deliver your specialty subject to your learners. Yes, you are more than a communicator. Much more! You are a teacher!

DEVELOPING YOUR LEARNING RELATIONSHIP

2

DISCOVERING THE PRINCIPLES OF TEACHING

If you think back to your learning experiences, you will discover many of the principles of effective communication. You learned these principles from an effective teacher. Your teacher provided you with a model of an effective communicator. You benefited from being helped by her or him. You learned from his or her experience in living and learning. The teacher worked both to shape your learning practices and to make you an effective communicator. Let us look at some of these communication practices.

UNDERSTANDING THE
LEARNING RELATIONSHIP

Perhaps most important, your mentor helped you to recognize the critical nature of the learning relationship. You came to realize that if real learning is to take place, it will be because the teacher-learner relationship is a fully human relationship: a relationship between human beings. One of them more knowledgeable in some areas, to be sure—the teacher; the others less knowledgeable in some areas—the learners. But a fully human relationship, nevertheless. The teacher serves as a guide on the most exciting, the most important voyage possible: a voyage to new growth and learning. As a guide, the teacher points out to learners the pitfalls and obstacles which past human history has revealed— and points out, too, the specific strategies and skills which represent the best that human growth has achieved. The teacher stands at the juncture of today's capabilities and tomorrow's risks and promises!

PREPARING YOURSELF FOR THE
LEARNING RELATIONSHIP

In this regard, you organize your efforts to facilitate the development of a constructive learning relationship with the learners. You organize the classroom to maximize learning activities. You are, indeed, wise to include yourself as part of the learners' learning environment. Accordingly, you appear and behave in ways that are appropriate to learning. You present yourself and your knowledge in an exciting manner, recognizing fully that the learners share the excitement of the teacher for the subject matter.

ATTENDING PHYSICALLY TO YOUR LEARNERS

You understand the necessity of being physically involved in your teaching. Simply stated, teachers are more likely to be involved if they are physically active. After all, you recognize that when Ben or Sara or Theo sit at their desks without moving or speaking, chances are they're really worlds away from the classroom. To be fully involved is to be active! You translate this principle into a program. You circulate throughout the classroom, a basic rule which you rarely break. In each and every class, you continually move about the room. You make it a point to walk by every child during every class period. In this manner, you energize your own learning program.

13

OBSERVING AND LISTENING
TO YOUR LEARNERS

You do not circulate around the room merely to be active and physically involved. You also circulate because you recognize the need for teachers to hear and see as much as possible. You understand deeply the principle that the teacher's attentiveness facilitates the learners' attentiveness. Learners attend to their teachers in much the same manner that their teacher attends to them. Accordingly, as you circulate around the room, you approach and look at each of the learners with whom you are talking. You address your learners fully so that you may observe each learner and so that each may observe you fully. You listen carefully to each learner's expression and expect, in turn, that he or she will listen to your expression. You are impressed by your recognition that much of what you know about your learners is a function of what you have observed in their behavior and heard in their expression. There is a difference between the child who is slumped at his desk and the child who sits erect, eyes bright and excited. There is a difference, too, between the listless *"What was the question?"* and the eager *"I know, I know!"*

RESPONDING TO YOUR LEARNERS

You are also impressed by the recognition that what you have to say to the learners influences their learning. It simply makes good sense to you that your learners will involve themselves most with you when you are responding directly to them. This means that you should respond in some informative way to every learner expression that is directed toward you. At a minimum, your responses should involve yourself in the first person: to *"How about* **that** *Mr./Ms._____?"* you might respond *"Why, I feel_____"* or *"I believe_____."* In this manner, you communicate your attentiveness to their verbal responses. At a maximum, your responses should respond to the learners: to *"There's just never enough time to get my homework done!"* you might initially respond *"You really feel pressured for time."* It is really not too much to expect for you to include the learner in your response.

UNDERSTANDING YOUR LEARNERS

Perhaps you are aware of the extensive evidence relating teacher level of responsiveness to learner academic achievement. Or perhaps it is just the feeling deep down inside of you that tells you that responding to the learners' feelings facilitates the teacher-learner relationship and, thus, the learners' achievement. Simply stated, teachers who understand learners are more potent influencers of learner behavior. Perhaps you have translated this principle into a basic rule whereby you make it a point to respond at least weekly to each learner's behavior with an expression that accurately individualizes that learner's unique experience: *"Marge, you really feel on top of the world because you finally licked those math problems, huh?"* Sometimes, after making a number of accurate responses, you find yourself able to go beyond the learners' expressions, to understand them and their needs in a much larger perspective or at a much deeper level. In addition to extensive experience with the learners, such responses require a large repertoire of interpersonal skills.

INITIATING WITH YOUR LEARNERS

Most of all, you are proud of your ability to help the learners achieve their learning goals. "This, after all, is what learning is all about," you conclude. With this in mind, you have developed your learning programs to achieve your learning goals. You have developed these programs as systematically as you can. You have tried not to leave out a step because you realize that doing so often causes a learner setback. You have tried to build as much success as you can into your programs. You have called upon all of your own resources as well as those around you to help your learners achieve their goals. Your learners are real people to you. And you want to make a real difference in their lives!

CHECKING YOURSELF OUT

You are committed to discharging all of the communicative responsibilities for which you are paid. You are dedicated to serving the people whom you are paid to serve—the learners, the parents and the community—as well as your fellow teachers. Again, discharging such extensive responsibilities requires an extensive repertoire of interpersonal skills. In turn, the development of an extensive repertoire of interpersonal skills requires systematic training. In the interest of developing ourselves and the learners whom we serve, let us pause now to check out the level of your interpersonal skills.

PRE-TRAINING HELPING ASSESSMENT

COMMUNICATING HELPFUL RESPONSES

In the course of a school year, learners present many different kinds of expressions: one day Lou is bouncing around the room like a jubilant rubber ball; the next day you have to speak to him twice before he even raises his eyes to look at you. How we deal with these expressions determines whether we help or harm the childrens' learning effort. We will now ask you to respond to one of these learner expressions. After you become expert in making judgements about what constitutes an effective interpersonal response, you will be able to come back and give your response a rating. In responding to the expressions, please formulate in writing the most helpful response which you might make. Assume that you have worked with this child several times previously. Write your response exactly as you would say it to the child. Do not describe what you would talk about. In the following exercise, a child comes to you, a teacher, and expresses this concern:

"I do my homework every night. But that stuff is just so stupid and boring that it's hard to do."

Please formulate the most helpful response that you might make to this learner.

Your response: _____

PRACTICING COMMUNICATING

It's not always easy to respond in the moment to a learner, or to anyone else for that matter. Perhaps you had some difficulty in responding to the first expression. So let's try another expression. Again, formulate the most helpful response that you might make to this learner. In this instance, a student comes to you and expresses this concern:

"You never give me a chance. You always pick someone else. You don't care about me."

Please formulate the most helpful response that you might make to this learner.

Your response: _____

_____

_____

_____

_____

_____

USING YOUR DISCRIMINATION SKILLS

By now you may realize how critical are the responses which we might make. You may also realize that many teachers have had very little preparation for communicating effective helping responses to these expressions. We will now give you an opportunity to get an index of your current ability to make judgements about effective communications. Being able to make accurate judgements or discriminations about what constitutes an effective communication will contribute to your being able to develop your own responses. You will receive immediate feedback on your ability to discriminate.

We will repeat the expression of the first student to the teacher. Then you will read five alternative responses to his expression. We will ask you to rate each of these responses on a scale from 1 to 5 as follows:

1—Very Ineffective
2—Ineffective
3—Minimally Effective
4—Very Effective
5—Extremely Effective

If you feel a response falls between two levels on the five-point scale, you may split the gap and rate 1.5, 2.5, 3.5 or 4.5. For example, if the response seemed to you to be between ineffective and minimally effective you would give it a 2.5. You may use a rating more than once.

DISCRIMINATING EFFECTIVE RESPONSES

Now read once again the expression of the first student, after which are five alternate teacher responses:

"I do my homework every night. But that stuff is just so stupid and boring that it's hard to do."

Please rate the following alternative teacher responses to this expression from 1 to 5:

Your Ratings   **Teacher Responses**

_____ 1. *"Don't give up because you have what it takes. I know because I was in the same position at one time in my life."*

_____ 2. *"You feel angry because that stuff is so stupid and boring."*

_____ 3. *"It'll work out—it always does."*

_____ 4. *"It makes you feel dumb because you can't handle the stuff and you really want to. Let's sit down and work out a study skills program. The first thing you have to do is survey any assignment that you have."*

_____ 5. *"You feel worried because you can't do it and you want very much to be able to."*

You should now have five ratings for the five different teacher responses to the learner expression.

PRACTICING DISCRIMINATING

You may now realize that discriminating the teacher's response effectively is no easier than communicating effectively yourself. You may recognize the fact that you do not have a well-developed way of assigning ratings to the responses. This is probably because no one has ever taught you to do so. At a later point in this book, you will be able to make those discriminations easily.

Try a second round. Rate the responses to the second student's expression to you.

"You never give me a chance. You always pick someone else. You don't care about me."

Please rate the following alternative responses to this expression from 1 to 5:

Your Ratings   **Teacher Responses**

_____   1. *"You're really discouraged because you want to be a part of this but you haven't been able to find a way."*

_____   2. *"You feel sad because I've let you down."*

_____   3. *"You haven't been working as hard as you should. You're just going to have to buckle down and do your work. All you have to do is work harder and I'll pick you."*

_____   4. *"What makes you feel that way?"*

_____   5. *"You're discouraged because you want me to like you but you haven't had the chance. Talking with me is the first step. Next you have to understand what behavior I expect from you."*

Again, you should have five different ratings for the five different responses to the learner expression.

LEARNING ABOUT
RESPONDING AND INITIATING

The responses you have just rated were varied according to the level of the teacher's responsiveness. Responsiveness simply means understanding how another person sees things. We are most responsive when our statements show we understand where the learner is and how she or he feels. Not just the condescending *"I know how you feel..."* but the convincing *"You feel_____."* For a response to be high in responsiveness, it must contain a feeling word such as *"happy,"* *"angry,"* *"sad"* or some other such term. If the response does not contain a feeling word, then it is low on responsiveness.

The responses were also varied according to initiative. Initiative means giving direction or guidance to another person. Initiative means helping the learners to understand where they want to be: not just *"You should do something (work harder, try more, etc.)"* but *"You want_____ so you should begin by_____."* For a response to be high in initiative, it must be high in direction. Sometimes this is in the form of advice—for example "do this"—or in the form of encouragement to continue in pursuit of their goals. Sometimes, it is in the form of helping the learners to understand where they want to go and how to get there.

Responsiveness and initiative are the two basic dimensions of interpersonal communication.

CHECKING OUT YOUR DISCRIMINATIONS

By now you may be eager to get an idea of how well you did in rating the teacher responses. We will give you feedback on your ability to discriminate effective from ineffective responses.

Trained raters, who have demonstrated the validity of their ratings in studies of teaching, rated each of the teacher responses on their level of responsiveness and initiative. Then they gave an overall numerical rating on effectiveness. These ratings are listed in the table below. As you can see, the statements receiving the highest rating (5.0) are those containing specific feeling words and providing specific direction. The lowest-rated statements reflect neither the learner's own feeling nor any real direction. You may now wish to determine your discrimination score.

Learner Expressions	Teacher Responses	Ratings
I	1	2.0
	2	3.0
	3	1.0
	4	5.0
	5	4.0
II	1	4.0
	2	3.0
	3	2.0
	4	1.0
	5	5.0

OBTAINING YOUR DISCRIMINATION SCORE

You may use the table of ratings to determine your discrimination score as follows:

1. Without regard to whether the difference is positive or negative, write down the difference between each of your numerical ratings and each of the trained raters' numerical ratings.

2. Add up the difference scores for each rating. You should have 10 difference scores, since there were two learner expressions and five alternate teacher responses to each expression.

3. Divide the total of the difference scores which you obtained in step 2 by the total number of ratings, 10. The result is your discrimination score.

SAMPLE

Learner Expressions	Teacher Responses	Ratings	Your Ratings		Difference (Deviation from Raters)
			1) Subtract		
I	1	2.0 -	4.0	=	2.0
	2	3.0 -	2.0	=	1.0
	3	1.0 -	3.0	=	2.0
	4	5.0 -	3.0	=	2.0
	5	4.0 -	2.0	=	2.0
II	1	4.0 -	2.5	=	1.5
	2	3.0 -	2.0	=	1.0
	3	2.0 -	4.0	=	2.0
	4	1.0 -	3.0	=	2.0
	5	5.0 -	2.5	=	2.5

2) Total = 18.0

3) Divide $\dfrac{18.0}{10}$ = 1.8 *Interpersonal Skills Discrimination Score*

Learner Expressions	Teacher Responses	Ratings	Your Ratings		Difference (Deviation from Raters)
			1) Subtract		
I	1	2.0	- _____	=	_____
	2	3.0	- _____	=	_____
	3	1.0	- _____	=	_____
	4	5.0	- _____	=	_____
	5	4.0	- _____	=	_____
II	1	4.0	- _____	=	_____
	2	3.0	- _____	=	_____
	3	2.0	- _____	=	_____
	4	1.0	- _____	=	_____
	5	5.0	- _____	=	_____

2) Total = _____

3) Divide $\dfrac{\rule{1cm}{0.15mm}}{10}$ = _____ *Interpersonal Skills Discrimination Score*

RECEIVING FEEDBACK

The average teacher who has not had systematic training in the responsive and initiative interpersonal dimensions, usually differs one (1.0) to one and one-half (1.5) levels from the raters' ratings. This is really not good since it means that where the trained raters rate an item at level 3.0, the teacher might rate the item at 4.5 or 1.5. You are rating as *"Highly Effective"* or *"Highly Ineffective"* a response that the trained rater rates as *"Minimally Effective."* A half a level deviation from rater ratings is considered a good discrimination score. This means that where the rater rates an item at level 3.0, the teacher might rate the item between 2.5 and 3.5. Both are near the minimally effective ratings of the rater. When you have completed the work in this book, you will deviate one half (.5) level or less from the trained raters' rating. Generally, people tend to be least accurate with responses which are low in responsiveness and high on initiative— *"You're just going to have to buckle down and do your work!"*—the Low-High Response. This is because, in our society, advice is often equated with helping. However, as our ratings indicate, understanding is more important than advice. Advice without understanding is often of limited value because, while it may respond to where the learners want to go (or more precisely, to where the teacher thinks the learners should go), it does not take into consideration where they are. You simply cannot get to a goal if you do not know where you are starting! You cannot help Carlos or Sara or Sam or Franny to be a better learner until you have first helped them see where they are in terms of their present strengths and weaknesses. It is like starting a journey to a particular destination without knowing your starting point. You simply cannot plot the course. Understanding without advice, on the other hand, has some minimal value because it at least responds accurately to where the learners are. You may wish to look at your ratings to determine where you were closest to the trained raters' ratings. You may also wish to look at your ratings to determine where you were farthest from the raters' ratings.

UNDERSTANDING THE REASON
FOR THE RATINGS

Now perhaps you are ready for a further explanation of the rating system. You may wish to have at least a tentative understanding of how the ratings were made by the raters. An explanation will also serve as preliminary training in discrimination. Later, you will receive more extensive training.

For the moment, let us say that high responsiveness simply means a feeling word was used by the teacher in her response to the learners' expressions. The teacher responded to where the learners were. Low responsiveness means that no feeling word was used in the teacher response. The teacher did not respond to where the learners were.

High initiative means that explicit direction was present in the form of telling the learners what to do or in showing them where they were going. The teacher responded to where the learners wanted to be. Low initiative indicated that no such direction was present. The teacher did not respond to where the learners wanted to be.

The following numerical scale may be used for rating the overall level of responsiveness and initiative.

Level of Dimensions

Responsiveness	Initiative	Ratings
Low	Low	1.0
Low	High	2.0
High	Low	3.0
High	High	4.0
High	High+	5.0

UNDERSTANDING A LOW RESPONSIVE LOW INITIATIVE RESPONSE

If you will look at each of the responses rated at 1.0—low on responsiveness and low on initiative, i.e., teacher response No. 3 on page 20 and teacher response No. 4 on page 21, you will see that neither of the responses contains a feeling word. They did not respond to where the learners are. Understanding how a person feels is the most important part of understanding. Therefore, both the responses are low in responsiveness. None of the responses contain any direction either. They do not respond to where the learners want to be. They are just comments or questions about things. In neither case does the response guide the learners toward something they can do to resolve their problem. After all, when was the last time that a response like *"Ah, don't worry about things so much!"* really helped you solve a personal problem?

27

UNDERSTANDING A LOW RESPONSIVE HIGH INITIATIVE RESPONSE

If you will look at the responses judged low in responsiveness and high in initiative and rated at 2.0, i.e., teacher response No. 1 to the homework problem and teacher response No. 3 to the favoritism problem, you will find that neither of these contains a feeling word either. They do not respond to where the learners are. But they both contain direction and/or encouragement in the form of something the learners could try to help them resolve their problems. In this respect, they do respond to where the learners want to be. Because understanding is lacking, the advice might not be the best; but at least the learners have something to try.

UNDERSTANDING A HIGH RESPONSIVE LOW INITIATIVE RESPONSIVE

If you now turn your attention to the responses considered to be high in responsiveness and low in initiative and rated at 3.0 or minimally effective level, i.e., teacher response No. 2 to the first problem and teacher response No. 2 to the second problem, you will find that all of these responses contain a feeling word. Both teacher responses respond to where the learners are. This is a good start toward communicating understanding. After all, when someone says to us *"You really look depressed,"* at least we know he or she is seeing and hearing the *"real"* us! However, none of the responses contains any direction or guidance. Neither teacher response responds to where the learners want to be. They simply show that the teacher understands where the learners are. The teacher's understanding of the learners' feelings and the reason why they feel the way they do are communicated. The evidence shows that understanding is more basic than advice and the scale scores reflect this.

UNDERSTANDING A HIGH RESPONSIVE HIGH INITIATIVE RESPONSE

If you look at the responses judged to be high in responsiveness and high in initiative and rated at 4.0, i.e., teacher response No. 5 to the first expression and teacher response No. 1 to the second expression, you will note that all of the responses contain a feeling word responding to where the learners are; but they also have direction and guidance in them, responding to where the learners want to be. The teacher response to the first student demonstrates that she understands how the learner feels, *"worried";* but she also provides guidance and direction by recognizing and bridging the gap between where the learner is, not being able to *"handle it,"* and where he wants to be, being able to *"handle it."* The teacher response to the second student communicates to the learner that she knows how the learner feels, *"discouraged."* Then she goes on to provide guidance and direction by identifying the step needed to bridge the gap between where the learner is, not feeling *"liked,"* and where she wants to be, *"liked"* by the teacher.

UNDERSTANDING A COMPLETE RESPONSE

Finally, if you look at the responses judged to be high on responsiveness and even higher on initiative and rated at 5.0, i.e, teacher response No. 4 to the homework expression and teacher response No. 5 to the favoritism expression, you will note that the responses contain both a feeling word that responds to where the learners are and an understanding of where the learners want to be. In addition, these teacher responses contain the initial attempts to develop a step for helping the learners get from where they are to where they want to be. In both instances, the teacher is ready to sit down and attempt to develop a program with or for the learner.

31

UNDERSTANDING RESPONSIVE AND INITIATIVE DIMENSIONS

With your new discrimination skills, you now have a preliminary ability to make discriminations of effective communications. You may now wish to check over your own communications. Just see if you had a word that reflected the feeling of the learners. Answer the question, *"Did you respond to where the learners were?"* Look to see if you gave some kind of direction or guidance. Answer the question *"Did you respond to where the learners wanted to be?"* Answer the question *"Did you help the learners to get from where they were to where they wanted to be?"* Many teachers are low on responsiveness and high on initiative on a majority of their responses. That is, they seek to give advice without communicating a basic understanding of the learners' frame of reference. You have now had a chance to learn to discriminate the critical dimensions of communicating, the responsive and initiative dimensions of interpersonal skills. In the following pages, you will learn to communicate effectively with these interpersonal skills.

PRE-TRAINING
INTERPERSONAL
OVERVIEW

HELPING YOUR LEARNERS EXPLORE

Your interpersonal skills will facilitate the learners' learning of the material involved. In order to learn, the learners must first have the opportunity to explore themselves. They explore themselves in relation to themselves. They explore themselves in relation to you. They explore themselves in relation to their world. In learning, they explore themselves in relation to the learning material. They try to find out **who they are** or **where they are** in relation to the learning material: *"I hate English because all the books we have to read are long and boring"; "I like math class because the teacher doesn't call on me unless I raise my hand."*

Phases of Learning

I

Learning Skills	**Exploring**
	where they are

FACILITATING EXPLORATION

Take a look at your learners as they approach a new learning task. They will begin their learning process by exploring. Lynn flips through the entire workbook before starting page 1; Raul examines all the pictures on the bulletin board before taking his seat. You will watch your learners examine the parts of the new learning. They will want to learn how the parts fit together. It is necessary for your learners to investigate how the new learning works.

You will listen to your learners, too, as they are introduced to the new learning. The learners will ask themselves, each other and you these questions.

"What's this?"

"Where does this go?"

"Is this right?"

It is up to you, their teacher, to help your learners examine where they are in relation to the new learning. You use your interpersonal skills with your learners so that they ask the questions they need to answer to find out where they are.

HELPING YOUR LEARNERS UNDERSTAND

Exploration prepares the learners for understanding. Learner understanding involves developing a perspective of **where they are** in relation to **where they want to be**. Frank wants to be able to improve his reading speed so he'll have more free time for athletics; Thelma wants to excell in a biology course because she's thinking about going pre-med in college. Again, understanding involves the learners in relation to themselves, in relation to you, in relation to their world. In relation to the learning material, it means that the learners know where they want to be. In other words, they set goals for their learning.

Phases of Learning

	I		II
Learning Skills	Exploring	➤	Understanding
	where they are		where they are in relation to where they want to be

PROMOTING UNDERSTANDING

You have helped your learners to explore. They are ready to understand where they are in relation to the new learning. The learners will understand the parts of the new learning in relation to what they know and what they want to know. Their understanding of how the parts fit together is critical when it comes to setting the learning goals for what they want or need to learn. And you, their teacher, can help your learners understand what they need to learn. Then you will hear your learners say as they begin to understand:

"I see how that part works. Now, I'll try this part."

"I know this but I've got to learn that."

"I think I can do it."

HELPING YOUR LEARNERS TO ACT

Understanding prepares the learners for acting. The learners must act upon their understanding in order to demonstrate that learning has occurred. Learner action involves the learners acting upon **how to get** from **where they are** to **where they want to be**. Again, action involves the learners in relation to themselves, to you and their world. In relation to the learning material, it means that the learners have acted to achieve their learning goals.

Phases of Learning

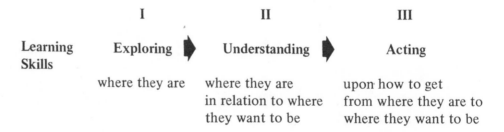

	I	**II**	**III**
Learning Skills	**Exploring**	**Understanding**	**Acting**
	where they are	where they are in relation to where they want to be	upon how to get from where they are to where they want to be

SUPPORTING ACTION

Your learners have explored the new learning. They have investigated the parts of the learning and how these parts fit together. They understand what they know and what they need to know. Then you will hear your learners say:

"I can do that!"
"Let me try!"
"It's my turn!"

Now they are ready to act with what they know to learn what they need to know. They anticipate the new learning and growth that will accompany their action. And you are there to maximize their learning in this action phase.

ATTENDING PREPARES YOU
AND YOUR LEARNERS

In Chapter Three, Involving Your Learners in Learning—Attending Skills, you will be introduced to one of the first skills which you need to teach effectively. You will learn the **attending skills** that make a helpful teacher-learner relationship possible. Before anything else is possible, you must **prepare** the learners for **involving** themselves in the learning relationship. In order to do this, you must communicate to your learners your full and undivided attention. This means that you must **attend physically** to your learners' needs, adopting specific actions to reflect your genuine concern, your internal *"I care"* attitude. You must **observe** their behavior: Leroy's woeful, tear-streaked expression; Janice's barely-repressed excitement over being elected to class office. You must **listen** to their verbal expressions: Linda's *"How come you never call on me?"* in counterpoint to Ian's *"How come you're always calling on me?"* Your attending skills will motivate the learners to invest themselves in the learning process. Learner involvement prepares them for exploring where they are in relation to the learning material.

Teacher: **Helping Skills**   Attending

POSITIONING COMMUNICATES ATTENTIVENESS

There are many ways that you attend to your learners. You face the learners so that you can see and hear all of them. In addition, you may move about the classroom so that you are physically closer to more of your students. When you are attending fully to your learners, you will say to yourself:

"Look at Mary scowling. She must need some help."

"What is John muttering under his breath? Does he want to ask a question?"

"Susan has finished. Let me check her work."

With a small group of learners, you position them in a semicircle around you. You may be seated so that you can observe and listen more fully to each member of the group: this way you can see all of Hank, not just the top of his head, as when he sits in a row behind Paulette. When one of your learners needs your help, you move to her or him so that you can attend to that learner. You lean toward the learner so that you can see and hear everything the learner says and does.

RESPONDING FACILITATES EXPLORING

In order to facilitate learners' exploration of where they are in relation to the learning material, you must respond to their experience. In Chapter Four, Helping Your Learners Explore Their Learning Experience—Responding Skills, you will be introduced to the key interpersonal dimension. In responding, you enter the learners' frames of reference. You see the world through their eyes. You get a grasp of where they are *"coming from,"* particularly in terms of their history of learning experiences. The effective teacher shies away from the self-centered *"You shouldn't get angry with Phil just because he got a better grade"* and responds in a nonjudgmental fashion instead—*"You feel pretty angry because Phil got a higher grade"* to communicate real understanding of the learner and her or his experience. All learning, you acknowledge, begins with the learners' frames of reference. Accordingly, you must respond to their **experience**, at least at the level that they have expressed it. You must respond to the **feeling** they have expressed. You must respond to the **meaning** or the reason for the feeling. Learner exploration prepares the learners for understanding where they are in relation to where they want to be.

⌐ **Phases of Learning**

Teacher:	**Helping Skills**	Attending	▶ Responding
Learners:	**Learning Skills**		Exploring

COMMUNICATING BY RESPONDING

Attending to your learners makes it possible for you to respond to your learners. Teacher responding is a skill which helps your learners to learn more efficiently. When your learners are having trouble mastering a new skill, you still acknowledge their feelings and experience. Responding to frustrated learners, you might say: *"You feel badly because this work is too hard."* Then your learners can explore their problem.

"Yes! We feel badly."

"Yes! The work is too hard!"

"Why is the work so hard?"

Then your learners are ready for more of your helping skills.

PERSONALIZING FACILITATES UNDERSTANDING

In order to facilitate the learners' understanding of where they are in relation to where they want to be, you must understand the learners at levels beyond those they have expressed. In Chapter Five, Helping Your Learners Understand Their Learning Experience—Personalizing Skills, you will be introduced to the understanding that flows from responding. You enter the learners' frames of reference so that you can understand where they want to go. Leslie's really worried because her grades will never get her into a good college; Sue feels panicky because her typing course has been her one good subject and now her grades are down in that course and she doesn't know whether she can still get a job after graduation. You see the world through their eyes so that you can grasp their hopes, their aspirations, their ambitions, their goals. All learning, you acknowledge, is dependent upon the learners' motivation to achieve their goals. You help the learners to understand where they want to be by **laying a base** of responses to their experiences. You then help them to **personalize** their experience by relating the learners' expressions to themselves. Finally, you personalize the learners' understanding of where they are in relation to where they want to be. Learner understanding prepares the learners for acting upon how to get from where they are to where they want to be.

Phases of Learning

Teacher: **Helping Skills**   Attending ▶ Responding   Personalizing

Learners: **Learning Skills**   Exploring   Understanding

COMMUNICATING BY PERSONALIZING

After you have responded to your learners' feelings and experience, you are ready to personalize their learning problem. You may say *"You feel mixed up because you don't know what these new words mean."* Then your learners can understand their problem. You have helped them understand what is missing in the learning experience. And they may respond to you as they begin to understand.

"We feel really mixed up!"

"We don't know what you're talking about."

"What do those words mean?"

YOUR INITIATING FACILITATES
THE LEARNERS' ACTION

In order to facilitate the learners acting to get from where they are to where they want to be, you must **initiate.** In Chapter Six, Helping Your Learners Act upon Their Learning—Initiating Skills, you will be introduced to the program-development skills that bring the process to a conclusion. You establish goals so that you may help the learners develop ways to achieve their learning goals. All learning, you acknowledge, depends upon the learners' demonstration of an increment in their performance: not just *"they're doing better in reading"* but *"their reading rate has improved to the point where they can handle their assignments in under 20 minutes."* You facilitate learner performance or action by developing programs. You develop programs that include the **goals** that reflect the learners'

understanding of where they want to be: *"Your goal is to spend no more than 30 minutes a night on any one homework assignment and still keep a 'B' average."* You develop programs that include the **first step** that comes from the learners' exploration of where they are: *"your first step is to list all the assignments you have due this week."* You develop programs that move in a **step-by-step** manner from the first step to the learning goal: *"Here are the five steps you need to take to reach your new goal."* Learner action prepares the learners for recycling the learning process. When the learners act, they receive feedback which stimulates further exploration, more accurate understanding and more effective action.

Phases of Learning

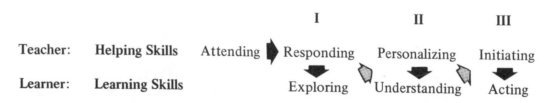

			I	II	III
Teacher:	**Helping Skills**	Attending	Responding	Personalizing	Initiating
Learner:	**Learning Skills**		Exploring	Understanding	Acting

COMMUNICATING BY INITIATING

Once your learners understand what they need to know in order to master the new skill, you can initiate what they need to learn. You initiate with a learning program which corrects these deficits in your learners. For example, if your learners did not know the vocabulary of the new skill, you might have them use their dictionaries to write the definitions of the new terms. Then you could have the learners use these definitions orally as they describe the new skill. Your learners are acting on their deficits when they define and use the new vocabulary. As your students act, you will hear them say:

"So that's what that word means."
"Now, we know what to do."
"See! We did it!"

TEACHING SKILLS ARE GUIDED BY LEARNER ACHIEVEMENT

The guiding theme throughout this book will be the phases of learners' learning-exploring where they are—understanding where they are in relation to where they want to be—and acting upon how to get from where they are to where they want to be. In using your helping skills, you will be guided by your effectiveness in achieving these phases of learners' exploration, understanding and action. The teaching skills which you learn will be shaped by your effectiveness in achieving the learners' learning goals. You'll help all your learners—all the Cliffords and Juanitas and bug-eyed, freckle-faced Aarons—get where they really want and need to be in terms of real growth and new capabilities.

47

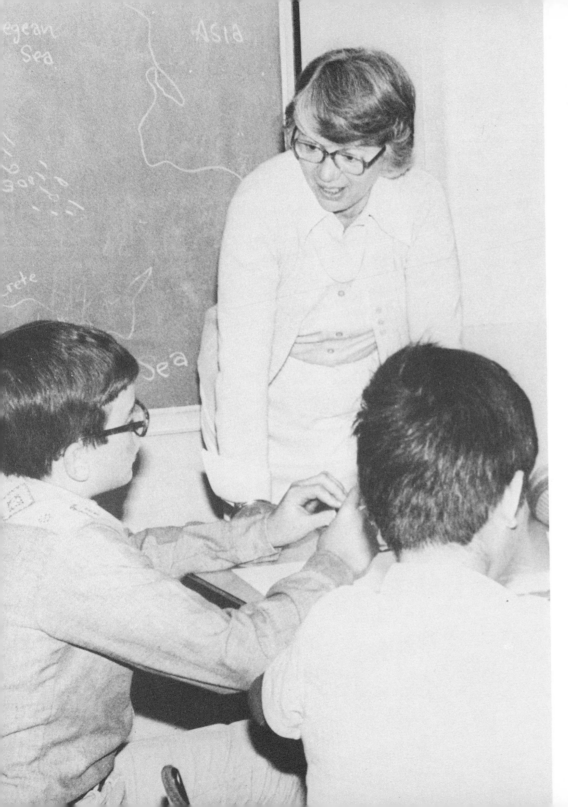

INVOLVING YOUR LEARNERS IN LEARNING —ATTENDING SKILLS

3

EXPERIENCING ATTENDING

You can recall the classroom vividly. As a learner, you sat in neatly ordered rows facing the teacher and the chalkboard, with her desk facing the middle row of seats. The teacher's desk! Oh, yes, the teacher's desk! It always seemed to stand there between you and the teacher. Even when you raised your hand and approached the desk, there was always a corner of it between you and the teacher. And she just glanced sideways at you to answer your question. She never really faced you fully. Except when you got into trouble. Then she got up out of her chair fast and hurried to your seat to reprimand you. It seems you always got the most attention when you were bad. Attention meant punishment.

LEARNING ATTENDING SKILLS

Attending is the first skill of teaching. Attending simply means that the teacher is attending physically to her learners and observing and listening to them. Attending is a pre-condition of helping and teaching. Attending communicates the teacher's interest in the learners and thus serves to involve the learners in the learning process. It also serves to lay the basis for responding to the learners' frames of reference in such a way as to facilitate the learners' exploration. In short, your attending says to each individual learner, *"I'm right here with you, I'm paying attention, I really do care."* At the same time, it allows you to say to yourself, *"I see each of them. I see how they look and act, I hear what they say and how they say it. I'm really getting to know them as individuals!"* Before we begin the attending module, let us check out the level of your attending skills.

PRE-TRAINING
ATTENDING ASSESSMENT

USING ATTENDING SKILLS

The learners who make up your classes are as varied as the teachers who have taught them. To be sure, in some ways they may be more differentiated. Some will make it in their lives. They will learn to live effectively. Not necessarily in terms of material wealth or social status but at a more profound and meaningful level. They will make it by actualizing their own full potential in careers from laborer to scientist; by establishing mutually beneficial relationships with others in marriages, family situations, everyday encounters; in short, by taking control of their own lives and making the most they can of these lives—for better rather than for worse!

How we attend to these learners determines the direction of their development. We will now ask you to employ one set of your attending skills. We will ask you to position yourself in a sitting position to effectively help a learner. **Position yourself exactly as you would to help someone else.** Do not describe what you would do. Record how you position your body.

In the following exercise, position yourself in a sitting position to help the learners pictured to the left.

USING YOUR DISCRIMINATION SKILLS

You may already realize how critical your attending behavior is. How you attend can help make the process go or hold it back right from the beginning. You may also realize that, as critical as this behavior is, no one has ever taught you directly how to demonstrate this behavior most effectively. We will now give you an opportunity to get an index of your current ability to make judgements about effective teacher attending behaviors. Being able to tell visually what an attentive person looks like will make it easier for you to increase your own attentiveness. You will receive immediate feedback on your ability to discriminate.

Let us view once again the learners to whom you attended. Then you will view five alternative attending behaviors to the learners. We will ask you to rate each of these behaviors on a scale from 1 to 5 as follows:

1–Very Ineffective
2–Ineffective
3–Minimally Effective
4–Very Effective
5–Extremely Effective

If you feel a behavior falls between two levels on the five-point scale, you may split the gap and rate 1.5, 2.5, 3.5 or 4.5. For example, if the behavior seems to you to be between minimally effective and very effective, you should give it a 3.5. You may use a rating more than once.

51

Your Ratings

Teacher Behaviors

_____ 1.

_____ 2.

_____ 3.

_____ 4.

_____ 5.

DISCRIMINATING ATTENDING BEHAVIORS

Now let us look at five alternative ways of attending to a classroom of learners. Please rate the following alternative teacher attending behaviors from 1 to 5.

CHECKING OUT
YOUR DISCRIMINATIONS

Since you may want to get some idea of how well you did in rating teacher attending behaviors, we will give you feedback on your ability to discriminate effective from ineffective attending behaviors.

Trained raters who have demonstrated the validity of their ratings in studies of teaching rated each of the teacher attending behaviors according to the level of attention which it gave the learner. These ratings are listed in this table.

You may determine your discrimination score by the following calculations: (1) obtaining the absolute difference between each of your numerical ratings and each of the raters' numerical ratings; (2) adding the difference scores; (3) dividing by the total number of ratings or 5. The result is your discrimination score.

Teacher Attending Behaviors	Ratings	Your Ratings	Difference *(Deviations)*
1	2.0	— _____	= _____
2	4.0	— _____	= _____
3	1.0	— _____	= _____
4	3.0	— _____	= _____
5	5.0	— _____	= _____

$$\text{Total} = \frac{\rule{2cm}{0.4pt}}{5} = \rule{2cm}{0.4pt}$$

Attending Discrimination Score

LEARNING ABOUT ATTENDING

Now perhaps you are ready for further exploration of the ratings. You may wish to have at least a tentative understanding of how the ratings were made. An explanation will also serve as preliminary training in discrimination or rating. Ratings of level 3.0 or above simply indicated that the teachers were attending to the learners in the respect that they postured themselves to give the learners their attention. Ratings below level 3.0 indicated that the teacher was not attending to the learners. When attending as in illustrations 2, 4 and 5, the teachers are at least making eye contact. They communicate increasing interest in the learners by leaning slightly toward the learners in illustration 2 and by decreasing the distance to the learners in illustration 5. There are many more variations of nonattending behaviors than attending behaviors. In illustration 3, we see the teacher who is writing on the blackboard or doing something without attending to the students. She attends only to her content. In illustration 1, we see the teacher who is only partially attending. Although squared off with the students, he leans away from the students and makes only occasional eye contact.

As we move on, you will learn how effective attending allows you to see and hear each learner more completely and accurately. For now, simply consider the way in which highly-rated attending positions can **show** learners that you're really with them—and, by the same token, how poor positions show only that your focus is elsewhere.

ATTENDING TRAINING

LEARNING TO ATTEND
TO YOUR LEARNERS

Attending skills consist of three sets of basic skills: **attending physically, observing** and **listening**. Attending physically simply means communicating to the learners that you are ready to provide them with your full and undivided attention. Observing means being able to *"see"* the physical behaviors and characteristics of the learners which give you cues to their experience: instead of a crowd of youthful faces, you note a frown, a grin, a pair of eyes that follow you in bright anticipation. Listening means being able to *"hear"* what has been said and how it has been said in order to understand the learners' experience: instead of a babble of voices, you pick out this learner's calm and assured comment, that one's hesitant, almost embarrassed question. Attending skills set the stage for responding in two basic ways. First, when you signal to the learners that you are ready to give them your full and undivided attention, they are more likely to start exploring themselves in relation to the learning material. Second, attending skills serve to give you all the cues you need to deliver your best responses which, in turn, set the stage for making you an effective teacher.

ATTENDING PHYSICALLY

LEARNING THE FOUR
DIMENSIONS OF ATTENDING

There are at least four basic dimensions of physical attending behavior. The first includes the **contextual or environmental** variables or how you prepare your setting for the learners. The second dimension incorporates **presentation** variables or how you present yourself to the learners. The third dimension of attending includes **postural** variables or how you posture yourself in relation to the learners. The fourth dimension of attending incorporates **visual** variables or the eye contact which you make with the learners. All of these dimensions converge to communicate to the learners that you are attending to them by giving your full and undivided attention.

ADDRESSING THE
LEARNING ENVIRONMENT

Contextual or environmental variables emphasize your preparation for receiving the learners. This dimension includes considerations of how attractive and functional the learning environment is. Are the seats placed so that you can attend to each learner individually? Are any spaces between seats wide enough so you can move in between them? Are all visually displayed materials relevant rather than distracting? If you have created a comfortable and stimulating environment, then you are attending to the learners' needs and increasing the probability of receiving their attention in return. You prepare the classroom so that each learner finds something which comes from her or his frame of reference. This dimension also addresses itself to how effectively you have prepared the learners for the classroom. This is particularly critical where you have no choice concerning the location or characteristics of your school or classroom. While you may not be able to affect your setting's accessibility and attractiveness to the learners, you may be able to increase your drawing power by relating your learners' unique home environments to your particular learning environment.

ADDRESSING YOUR PRESENTATION

Presentation variables emphasize how you present yourself to the students. There are at least two dimensions of presenting yourself. The first is your **appearance** or how you look to the learners. The second is your **behavior** or how you act with the learners. Appearance emphasizes your dress and grooming. Let it be said simply: your dress and grooming should reflect your functions as teacher. Both should be appropriate to your role as a teacher who has something to offer your learners; while you understand their frame of reference accurately, you are not one of them. Any props that detract from your essential teaching functions are dysfunctional and therefore inappropriate to teaching. We are reminded of an anecdote about a young teaching intern who tried to make it with the learners by dressing like them. At the end of his internship, the learners were heard to say *"He's an O.K. guy, but why does he have to dress so creepy?"* Your own learners, too, will take note of how you look. And while they may still have a lot to learn about reading or history or basic physics, chances are they already know a lot about genuineness and honesty. They know you're not the same as they are— and they don't expect you to dress the same! In this regard, your behavior is most critical. After all, you represent the model for what it is you are teaching. Let your learners see you present yourself fully and directly as an effective model for living, learning and working. Your behaviors should be devoted to this end —no more, no less! Your behaviors constitute the model for what it is they would become. Your behaviors constitute the means for their becoming. Give your learners the best you have in every moment. You will understand this dimension better when we observe the learners' presentation of themselves.

ADDRESSING YOUR POSTURE

Perhaps the most significant dimension of attending behavior involves the postural variables. There are two basic behaviors involved in posturing yourself to attend to a person in such a way as to communicate your full and undivided attention. First, you should face the person. In particular, you should face the person squarely—your left shoulder to her right shoulder and vice versa. This communicates your fullest attention and openness. Second, you should lean toward the person. When we are interested in something in front of us, we naturally lean forward: think of the person watching the end of a thrilling movie, sitting on the edge of her seat and leaning forward expectantly; or the learner who leans forward in his seat, anxious to respond to a question. If you are sitting, you may bend the whole upper part of your body toward the person. You should bend forward far enough so that your forearms rest on your upper legs when your feet are flat on the floor. If you are standing, you should also be squared off, leaning forward and close enough to touch the materials on the learner's desk.

ADDRESSING YOUR EYE CONTACT

Finally, visual variables emphasize the eye contact which you make with the learners. Through your efforts to maintain contact with the learners' eyes, the learners are aware of your efforts to make contact with them as individuals. In addition, your attending eyes will be the source of your richest learning concerning the learners. Does Roberto consistently look away? Does Lynn consistently meet your gaze? Is this learner challenging, that one interested, a third shy or unhappy? The observations which you make of the learners will allow you to make inferences concerning the learners' relationship to the learning materials. All of your future teaching activities are dependent upon your ability to posture yourself in order to make eye contact with the learner.

CHECKING OUT
YOUR ATTENDING BEHAVIORS

You may wish to assess yourself right now in terms of how well you are attending. You can test yourself out by just determining how well you are attending to the material being presented to you in this book. First **FREEZE** in position. Then ask yourself some questions. Are you facing the material squarely? Is the material turned off to one side or are you turned off to one side? Are you leaning toward the material or are you leaning back, maybe even with your feet up? Do you maintain steady eye contact with the book or do you keep looking around? These behaviors reflect whether you are really involved in what you are learning or whether you are maintaining distance between the learning material and yourself. Are you setting the stage for taking in what is being presented or not? You may use these same questions to study whether the learners are involved in the learning material which you are presenting to them.

PRACTICING ATTENDING BEHAVIORS

Here is a brief exercise in attending. Our task will be to practice attending while standing. The first step will be to stand directly opposite the person to whom you are going to attend. Stand so that you will be about three feet away after you lean fully forward.

The second step will be to assume an attending posture, facing the person squarely, leaning forward and establishing eye contact. Maintain this position for about 30 seconds. If you have a full length mirror, it is helpful to practice in front of the mirror so that you can see what you look like. You may also want to rehearse this with your family at home before trying to use it in school.

DROPPING OUT INEFFECTIVE ATTENDING BEHAVIORS

Here are some notes that may help to explain your attending behavior. When asked to attend, you may find that you assume a posture that is not consistent with our recommendations. Some of you will find that you assume the *"thinker's"* posture that you learned so well as learners. This is usually not a truly attentive posture because it concentrates more upon a symbolic expression of interest than upon really providing full and undivided attention to the learners. Or you may find that you tilt your head to communicate interest. Do not do this! One of the things that you want to communicate as a teacher is strength. Tilting your head takes away from this. Also, in your efforts to maintain eye contact you may sometimes find yourself chasing the learners with your eyes. If the learners want to drop their eyes or look away, let them do this. Attending means giving them their private moments as well as your full attention.

EMPHASIZING FUNCTIONAL ATTENDING BEHAVIORS

You may feel more comfortable in other positions. Some like to be relaxed and spread out, draped over a chair or with feet on the desk. Others like to be spontaneous and creative in the moment, doing their own thing. Still others are disposed toward chalk or pencil props and spend their time tossing them in the air. Finally, some feel most comfortable not viewing the learners, claiming they *"hear"* better when they cannot *"see."* Forget it! A guiding principle of teaching or any helping situation is this: **teaching is for the learners—not the teacher!** Consequently, you should do everything that you can to make a delivery to the learners. Attending is just the first step in your delivery program. If you cannot take it, you cannot make your delivery to the learners.

USING ATTENDING BEHAVIORS

On the other hand, some of you may feel concern that your attending behavior will make the learners uncomfortable. Sometimes it will, at least at first. We get so little undivided attention that it often makes us uncomfortable at first—especially since such attention has often been equated with trouble. In the past, haven't we, as teachers, tended to approach learners' desks when we were angry? Do you remember how your own stomach fluttered when, as a learner yourself, you saw the teacher marching down the aisle toward you? However, in this instance, attending is the first step in building a relationship. You are giving them your full and undivided attention in order to teach them and help them. If you think it is important to build a relationship with the learners, you should continue to attend, since attending will ultimately help you to do a better job of teaching and helping. If your attending behavior precipitates a small crisis, you will be equipped to help the learners through the crises with the other interpersonal skills which you will learn. The point is simply to give your learners complete and undivided attention when you talk with them. To do this, you approach the learners and use your attending skills while interacting.

It will help you to learn the attending skills if you practice attending in your everyday life activities. Practice attending behaviors during your daily conversations. Ask one or two people with whom you are comfortable for their reactions to your attending. You should find that they have noticed your increased level of attending.

PRACTICING ATTENDING TO LEARNERS

Now let us develop an attending exercise in the classroom. Now that you have practiced attending behaviors, it is time for you to translate your attending to the classroom. Here are some translations to classroom behavior.

First, you should continually circulate around the room as you talk, briefly attending to each individual.

Second, you should approach and attend to the learners whenever they are directly interacting with you. If you are at the chalkboard writing, a half-turn toward the learners communicates only half interest. Complete what you are writing, turn fully and approach the learners to whom you are talking.

PRACTICING ATTENDING PHYSICALLY

Now attend physically to a large group of learners in the classroom. Wherever you are in relation to the entire class or to groups of students, you should square with them. You can do this by placing yourself at the point of a 90-degree angle drawn from the corners of the learners to your extreme left or right. Make sure that all learners are incorporated within the boundaries of the legs of your triangle. That way you can attend physically to all of the learners: to Ernie in the extreme right corner as well as to Iris in the extreme left. You're showing that you care about all of them equally, not just the few who have ended up front and center. Remember, stand erectly and do not sit at or on your desk or hold yourself up by leaning against the wall. Always face the class or group of learners and lean slightly forward toward them. This way you will be sure to observe all of your learners.

OBSERVING

ATTENDING IN ORDER TO OBSERVE

One of the main purposes in attending to the learners is to **observe** them. When you face the learners squarely, you can observe them fully. When you lean forward or toward them, you can pick up the details of their appearance and behavior. When you make eye contact with them, you can focus with intensity upon their characteristics. What you observe in the learners is potentially a very rich source of cues for responding to them. You're not just looking in their general direction but really **seeing** them as individuals—people who may, today, be slightly or even dramatically different from the way they were yesterday. You observe the same dimensions in your learners that you emphasized in your own attending behavior: their context or environment; their presentation; their posture; their eye contact.

OBSERVING YOUR LEARNERS' CONTEXT AND ENVIRONMENT

Just as you addressed the contextual and environmental dimensions of your attending behavior as a teacher, so do you now address the contextual and environmental dimensions of the learner. You can observe how well the students have used and organized their environment to facilitate their learning. You can observe the students' context or environment in various sources: are their desks clean or graffiti-laden, their books serviceable or torn and smudged, their lockers organized or overflowing, their rooms at home effective living-working spaces or disaster areas, their cars functional or fantastical? This, of course, argues for periodic home visits by the teacher in order to observe the conditions of the home within which the learners operate. Most important, you can observe the people— expecially their peers and family—with whom your learners associate, for people are the most significant aspect of their environment. In particular, you can observe the presence or absence of constructive older role models for their identification and emulation.

OBSERVING YOUR
LEARNERS' APPEARANCES

Just as you addressed your own presentation so do you now observe the learners' presentation of themselves. Again, you can divide these observations into two basic categories, appearance and behavior. Observing the learners' appearance means seeing how the learners look. Appearance may refer to clothing and grooming or personal characteristics such as age, body build, race, sex and so on. Each distinguishing characteristic of the learners may provide you with the possibility of making an inference. These inferences, however, must always be checked later in interaction with the learners. For example, if you observe that your learners are dressed very neatly and conservatively in dark and tailored clothes, you may infer that their conservative dress reflects a conservative image which they would like to project. Similarly, if you find learners who are very well groomed or made-up, with clothes attractive and matching, you may infer that they care a lot about how they look. Such learners may be meticulous in other situations where they are viewed. Finally, if the learners are very large and muscular in build, you may infer that they experience lots of strength and that they have lots of reserve physical strength to draw on. These are just some illustrations on how you may observe the appearance of your learners and make inferences from their appearance. Each inference should be checked against subsequent information which might either support or contradict it.

OBSERVING
YOUR LEARNERS' BEHAVIORS

Observing learner behavior simply means seeing what the learner does behaviorally and making inferences from this behavior. The behavior may be voluntary or involuntary on the learner's part. For example, when the learners fidget a lot in their chairs, you may infer that they are nervous or edgy and, at a minimum, are not comfortable in the setting. When they blink and look down continuously, you may infer that they are embarrassed or ashamed of what is going on. When they attend to you with their heads up, you may infer that they are really involved and that they have a high energy level and perhaps are even emotionally strong. Behaviors which indicate energy level are among the most important we can observe. Given sufficient energy, almost any learning is possible. Without it, doing anything will be difficult. You know yourself how poorly you function when you haven't had enough sleep and/or nourishment. You know, too, how on your best mornings you feel as though you could lick any problem in the world—and probably could! In the moment, behaviors like attending postures indicate a high energy level while sagging, slumped behavior indicates low energy. In a life situation, you observe these cues as well as the learners' overall activity level. Both appearance and behavior cues aid you in determining how the learners may see themselves and what they value. In addition, noticing how much the learners are like you physically may also help you to know the degree to which you and they will experience things the same way. After all, simple differences in sex or race or background can signal potential differences in the ways people will experience and respond to things. In general, the more alike you and your learners are, the more you will tend to look at things the same way. This will be helpful when you are trying to identify their feelings and how they may be different from yours.

OBSERVING YOUR LEARNERS' POSTURES

One of the most obvious sets of cues in observing the learners is the same posturing behaviors which they can observe in you. For example, whether the learners face you or the subject material squarely or not will tell you a great deal about their level of attentiveness to what is being communicated. In addition, you may make some inferences concerning their past learning history. You may make inferences concerning their success or failure in previous learning experiences based upon whether they address you or the subject matter fully: Jon got an 'A' in English last year and is ready, willing and able to commit himself fully; Estelle, on the other hand, had trouble in several classes last year and now sits slumped and dejected in her seat. Whether or not the learners lean forward or toward you, the teacher or the subject matter will tell you a great deal about their level of interest and investment in learning. It will also tell you something about their past experiences and intense relationships with either people or material. It will tell you something about their current experience and relationship with you. Your modeling always serves as a rich source of learning for your learners.

OBSERVING YOUR
LEARNERS' EYE CONTACT

Whether the learners make and keep direct eye contact with you or the learning material will tell you something about the level and the intensity of their commitment to conquer the learning involved. Gwyn looks right at you, intent upon not missing a thing. Fred couldn't care less—his focus is on his friends Ben and Les who sit in the next row. In particular, the moments when they lose eye contact are significant moments which may be related to the specific learning involved. You may also make inferences concerning the learners' past history of success or failure when they focused with intensity upon the details of learning. Finally, you can observe how well your learners observe the dimensions of their environment that are relevant to their learning. You can observe whether they see significant material in the sharp relief necessary to maintain a broad perspective. You can observe whether they can add the fine detail necessary to bring the learning to culmination.

PRACTICING OBSERVING LEARNERS

Being an accurate observer of learners is perhaps the most important skill that a teacher can have, and yet because of the level of intensity that observing demands, it is a most difficult skill to conquer. You discover most of what you need to know about your learners from observing their behavior. You can use your verbal interaction with them later to check out the accuracy of your observations of their behavior.

Let us take a moment to practice this most critical and difficult skill. Try to recall your own behavior over the past five minutes. See if you can recall three specific behaviors— three things you've done that an observer might have noted—and draw an inference from each of these. Make at least one observation concerning the level of energy indicated by your behavior: for example, *"I supported my head on my hand while I read, which might mean a low level of energy."* Remember, energy level is perhaps the key observation you can make concerning the learners' potential for development. Accordingly, energy level is the key observation your learners will make of your potential to be with them.

Now take a look at yourself in the mirror and note three characteristics of your appearance and draw an inference from each of these: for example, *"I'm dressed well and am neatly groomed, which might indicate to others that I care about my appearance."* Spend some time with yourself or a partner in exploring the accuracy of your observations and the validity of your inferences. Reformulate your inferences and observations to reflect even more accurately your experiences.

DRAWING INFERENCES FROM APPEARANCE AND BEHAVIOR

Now let us make some translations of your observing behavior to the classroom. Pick out three children in your classroom and observe each of them as they read or practice the skills you are teaching them. Again, recognize that your attending behavior creates the conditions for your observing their behavior fully.

Write down three characteristics of each learner's appearance and three behaviors that you observed. Draw an inference from each of these. Include behaviors which indicate the energy level of each learner. (For example, maybe Jane has dark circles under her eyes; this would seem to indicate tiredness and a low level of energy. And she moves about the room slowly with her shoulders slumped, supporting the original inference.)

Student 1

Appearance	Inference
1. _____	1. _____
2. _____	2. _____
3. _____	3. _____

Behavior	Inference
1. _____	1. _____
2. _____	2. _____
3. _____	3. _____

Student 2

Appearance	Inference
1. _____	1. _____
2. _____	2. _____
3. _____	3. _____

Behavior	Inference
1. _____	1. _____
2. _____	2. _____
3. _____	3. _____

Student 3

Appearance	Inference
1. _____	1. _____
2. _____	2. _____
3. _____	3. _____

Behavior	Inference
1. _____	1. _____
2. _____	2. _____
3. _____	3. _____

PRACTICING OBSERVING
IN THE CLASSROOM

Now observe a large group of learners in the classroom. Look at the large group as a whole. Look for changes in the large group just as you look for changes in the appearance and behavior of individuals. Observe whether the students have the correct materials and how they are attending physically to these materials. Notice whether they are facing, squaring, leaning toward and making eye contact with the materials. That way you will be sure to observe all of your learners.

LISTENING

ATTENDING IN ORDER TO LISTEN

Just as attending behavior facilitates observing behavior, so observing facilitates listening behavior. Listening simply means hearing what the learners have said. Some teachers look as though they are listening when they assume an attending and observing posture, but they do not *"hear"* what the learners have said: *"Yes....right....uh huh ....O.K., could you repeat your question one more time?"* There are a number of things that you can do to help you listen more effectively. First, you can attend and observe the learners as we have been practicing. The more your attention is focused on the learners, the greater your chances of actually hearing them. Attending and observing will also help you to resist outside distraction.

Second, you can suspend your judgement in listening to the learners. Just try to hear what they are saying. Never mind whether Jess **should** or **should not** be worried about his assignment; instead, find out how he **does** feel right now! If you get caught up in your reaction to them, you will miss what they have been saying. Your reaction to the learners will only assume significance for the learners if they know that you understand where they are *"coming from."*

Third, know why you are there with the learners and what you are listening for. You should be listening for the important things the learners are saying about themselves. The weather and the ballgame are only important insofar as they tell you something about the learners themselves.

RECALLING YOUR
LEARNERS' EXPRESSIONS

You will probably never be called on in a teacher-learner relationship to repeat verbatim what the learners have said. Nevertheless, practicing listening verbatim will give you an experiential feel for how intense a close-listening process really is. Knowing exactly what the learners have said is also a first step toward being able to formulate an accurate response to them: you can't respond to Lori's thought or feeling, for example, until you know precisely what it is!

Here are some exercises that may help you to practice listening verbatim. First, have someone give you a stimulus expression for about 10 seconds. For most people, this is about two sentences: for example, *"I don't know why we have to keep reading this stuff! One book's just like the next."* If you do not have someone to work with, you can take the stimulus expression from the radio or TV.

Second, repeat what was said verbatim.

Delay your response to be sure that you are accurate. Use the first person just as if you were the person who recited the expression initially. Here it is helpful if you can possibly record what is being said, as this will give you more accurate feedback. Another alternative is to have a third party judge your efforts.

Third, practice the first two steps about 10 times.

Fourth, have a person make a longer statement or listen to the TV or radio for 30 seconds.

Fifth, capture the gist of what was being said during this 30 seconds. Use this format: *"You're saying_____."*

Sixth, check back with the person or recording to see if you have left out anything important. Practice doing this 10 times in preparation for responding.

PRACTICING LISTENING
TO YOUR LEARNERS

Now let us make some translations to the classroom. There are a number of opportunities to use your listening skills in the classroom. This will give you a chance to check yourself out in terms of how well you are hearing your learners. One way to check yourself out is to use a format that the child can check out. The child is asking a question. You might say, *"So, you're asking_____,"* and repeat the gist of what the child said. Or, you might say, *"If I understand you, then, you are asking_____"* and repeat the gist of what the child has said.

In the context of a class discussion you might say, *"So Susie, you're saying_____. How would you respond to that, Juan?"*

Finally, in the context of a presentation on film or by a student, you might say, *"Tom is saying_____. How do you feel about that, Thelma?"*

List at least one other situation in your classroom where you might comfortably repeat what has been said. Also list the format you could use. Practice repeating the gist of what has been said by people in your class at least twice a day for a week. You will constantly practice listening skills in learning to communicate effectively.

PRACTICING LISTENING
IN THE CLASSROOM

Now practice listening to a large group of learners in the classroom. Listen carefully for the questions your learners are asking, especially those involving any materials they might need to do their tasks. Listen for the feeling of the expressions they are making. Try to hear whether they are feeling *"up"* or *"down."* This will help to guide you in determining whether they are ready to get involved in the lesson or not. Listen for the quiet that will tell you whether your learners are ready to begin their learning tasks.

PRACTICING ATTENDING
FULLY IN THE CLASSROOM

Now put your skills in attending physically, observing and listening all together by attending fully in the classroom. That way your attentiveness will communicate your interest in and concern with your learners. In addition, your attentiveness will tell you what you need to know about your learners in order to teach them. By attending fully to your learners, you will involve them in the learning process. By attending and involving your learners, you will prepare yourself for responding to their experiences in learning.

MAKING APPLICATIONS OF ATTENDING

See if you can apply two or more translations of attending to the classroom. Consider the interactions between learners as well as between you and the learners. Now practice the five attending behaviors in your classroom. In addition to the general attending goals, try to make sure you attend fully to each learner once each day if you are teaching in the primary grades and once each week if you are a secondary teacher. You should find that the more you attend to the learners, the more attending behavior they engage in with you. As you devote more time to focusing on, observing and listening to the Angels, Eds, Ritas, Raouls and Sylvias who are your learners, they will begin paying closer attention to you. In other words, your learners will be involved in learning. Later on, you may want to teach them directly how to attend in learning.

POST-TRAINING
ATTENDING ASSESSMENT

USING YOUR ATTENDING SKILLS

Now let us make a post-training assessment of your attending behaviors. This time, we will ask you to position yourself in a standing posture to help the learners effectively. Position yourself exactly as you would to attend to the learners in a library scene. Record how you would position your body.

In the following exercise, position yourself in a standing posture to help the students pictured below.

DISCRIMINATING ATTENDING BEHAVIORS

Let us view the learners whom we attended. But this time, let us judge the student learning behaviors. Let us view the five alternative attending behaviors of the learners. We will ask you to rate each of the behaviors from 1.0 (very ineffective) to 5.0 (extremely effective) with 3.0 being minimally effective. Again, you may split the gap if you feel a behavior falls between two levels.

Your Rating

Student Behaviors

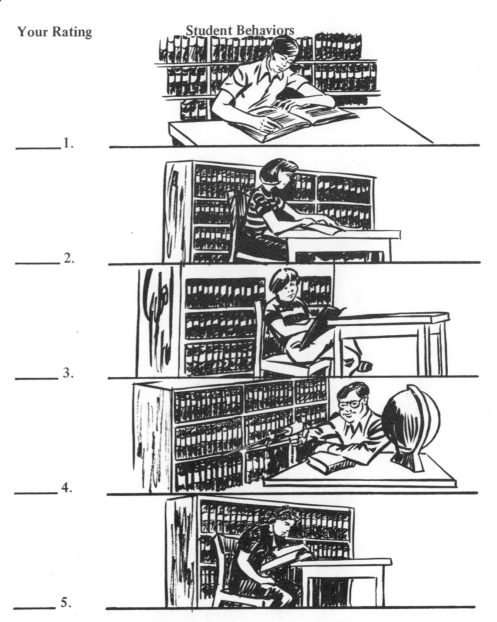

_____ 1.

_____ 2.

_____ 3.

_____ 4.

_____ 5.

CHECKING OUT YOUR
ATTENDING DISCRIMINATIONS

Again, the trained raters' ratings are listed in the table below. You may determine your discrimination score by obtaining your absolute deviations, adding them and dividing the total by 5. The result is your attending discrimination score. (For example, if you rated the first illustration 4.0, the second 3.5, the third 2.5, the fourth 1.5 and the fifth 4.0, your absolute deviation was a total of 2.0; dividing this by 5 yields a discrimination score of .4.)

Learner Attending	Ratings	Your Ratings		Differences *(Deviations)*
1	4.0	— _____	=	_____
2	3.0	— _____	=	_____
3	2.0	— _____	=	_____
4	1.0	— _____	=	_____
5	5.0	— _____	=	_____

Total = _____ = _____
5   *Attending Discrimination Score*

RECEIVING FEEDBACK

Some further feedback will help you to consolidate your learnings. Again, ratings of level 3.0 or above mean the student postured himself or herself to attend to the learning material. Ratings below 3.0 mean that they did not posture themselves effectively. The highest level of attending involves the learner attending physically, observing and reading the material. This means that the learner is squared off, making eye contact and has closed the distance to the learning material. Rated at level 5.0, Behavior 5 is the model for attending. Everything else falls short of the highest levels of involvement that lead to maximal learning. Accordingly squaring off, making eye contact and leaning only slightly forward is rated 4.0 (Behavior 1). Occasional eye contact is rated level 2.0 (Behavior 3), while nonattending behavior is rated at level 1.0 (Behavior 4).

UNDERSTANDING ATTENDING

You should have improved in your discrimination of attending behaviors. In this instance, your post-training discrimination of your observations of the learners' attending behaviors should have improved over your pre-training discrimination of the teachers' attending behaviors. Your discrimination score should be below one-half level deviation from the given ratings. If your discrimination score has not improved or is not below one-half level deviation, you should reread this chapter before proceeding in your interpersonal skills training. All the interpersonal skills that follow are dependent upon attending skills. You can develop your own scale for attending. Now that you have learned rating, you can rate your level of attending on the pre- and post-behavior tests. Again, your rating of your attending behavior should have improved significantly from before to after attending training. You are now ready to attend effectively to your students.

Level 1: Nonattending
Level 2: Partial Attending: Occasional eye contact
Level 3: Attending Minimally: Eye contact; squared off; erect
Level 4: Attending Intensely: Eye contact; squared off; learning forward
Level 5: Attending Maximally: Eye contact; squared off; closing the distance

Attending Skills

Pre-Training   **Post-Training**

_____Your Rating _____Your Rating

MASTERING ATTENDING

Once you have mastered attending skills, you have taken the first step toward effective teaching (level 2.0). Attending communicates to your learners that you are paying attention to what they say and what they do. When Denise starts distracting others around her by clowning, she will notice you approaching her desk. Denise is aware that you are preparing to attend to her. You have only used some of your attending skills and yet it will be enough to bring Denise back in line. When Larry moans about his math problems, you will lean toward him and make eye contact. Then he will know that you care if he can do the math. He knows that you are ready to help him. And when Sheila comes to you to complain about *"kids picking on her,"* you can focus your full attention on her. Then she will know that you are concerned about her.

Mastery of attending behaviors insures that you will be able to recognize the discipline problems that detract from your teaching. You will begin to explore what your learners need to learn. Your learners will know that you care about them. With effective attending, teaching is possible. Without effective attending, nothing is possible.

HELPING YOUR LEARNERS
EXPLORE THEIR LEARNING EXPERIENCE
—RESPONDING SKILLS

EXPERIENCING RESPONDING

You told everyone in school what had happened to you. The other kids' eyes widened and their mouths gaped with interest. Their successive questions gave further proof of their excitement. You grew still more involved in your subject matter as you answered their questions. To be sure, you asked some of your own of them: *"Do you think it could have been....?"* You really told your story quite well. You were quite proud of yourself. You searched the teacher's face for signs of approval. You heard only her voice as she quickly looked to another corner of the room: *"O.K., next."*

LEARNING RESPONDING SKILLS

Responding is really the first stage of interpersonal skills. Responding means communicating an understanding of the experience expressed by the learners: *"You're really excited about all the things you saw on your vacation, aren't you?"* Responding facilitates the learners' exploration of where they are in relation to themselves, you, learning material or their worlds in general. Responding lays the base for personalizing the learner's understanding. Before we begin the responding module, let us check out the level of your responding skills.

Teacher: **Helping Skills**   Attending ▶ Responding

Learner: **Learning Skills**   Exploring

PRE-TRAINING
RESPONDING ASSESSMENT

FORMULATING RESPONSES

The experiences expressed by learners run a full range of affect and content areas. You learn how Jimmy feels, what Jen thinks, what Ray did about his homework, where Howie would like to go to college. How you respond to these expressions is critical. If you communicate accurate understanding, then you and your learners may go on to work together to solve problems or achieve goals. If you do not communicate accurate understanding, you may not go on to work together to solve problems or achieve goals. How we respond to the learners' expressions will make the difference in whether they overcome or are overcome by obstacles, whether they work or fail to work effectively to achieve their learning objectives. We will now ask you to respond to one of these student expressions. In responding to the expression, please formulate in writing the response that communicates most accurately your understanding of the learners' experience at the level that they have expressed it. Write your response exactly as you would say it to the learner. Do not describe what you would talk about. In the following exercise, a student comes to you and expresses this concern.

"Sometimes she acts like she is my best friend and the next day she acts like she doesn't even know me!"

Please formulate the most accurate response that you can make to this student's expression.

Your response: _____

_____

_____

_____

_____

_____

_____

DISCRIMINATING RESPONSES

You may find some difficulty in making an accurate formulation. You now realize the meaning of the proverb *"Easier said than done."* You may also realize how critical is the response which you make. If you are accurate, you communicate that you understand the learner at the level that the learner has presented herself. If you are inaccurate, you either add to or subtract from the expression by the learner. If you are subtractive—*"Don't worry so much!"*—you may be harmful, taking away from some of the experience. If you are additive—*"I know just how inadequate you feel, and here's what you should do"*—you may not be helpful because you are premature. We will repeat the learner's expression. Then you will read five alternative teacher responses. We will ask you to rate these responses from 1.0 (very ineffective) to 5.0 (extremely effective) with 3.0 being minimally effective.

Now, read once again the expression of the same student after which you will read five alternative teacher responses. Please rate the responses from 1.0 to 5.0 with level 3 reflecting that response which most accurately captures the learner's experience. Split the gaps between levels as much as is appropriate.

"Sometimes she acts like she is my best friend and the next day she acts like she doesn't even know me."

Your Rating

_____ 1. *"I believe that you should not be her friend anymore."*

_____ 2. *"You feel sad."*

_____ 3. *"You feel that she doesn't treat you right."*

_____ 4. *"You feel hurt because she doesn't treat you right."*

_____ 5. *"I believe that you should go to her and speak to her since she matters so much to you."*

CHECKING OUT YOUR
RESPONDING DISCRIMINATIONS

Trained raters who have demonstrated the validity of their ratings in studies of teaching rated each of the teacher's attempts to respond accurately to the learner's experience. These ratings are listed in the table below. You may determine your discrimination score by obtaining your absolute deviations, adding them and dividing the total by 5. The result is your discrimination score.

Teacher Responses	Ratings	Your Ratings	Difference (Deviations)
1	1.5 −	_____ =	_____
2	2.5 −	_____ =	_____
3	2.0 −	_____ =	_____
4	3.0 −	_____ =	_____
5	2.0 −	_____ =	_____

Total = $\dfrac{\rule{2cm}{0.4pt}}{5}$ = _____

Responding Discrimination Score

RECEIVING FEEDBACK

You may wish to explore some of the ratings further. The rating of level 3.0 was assigned to Response 4 because it accurately reflected the feeling *("hurt")* and the reason for the feeling *("because she doesn't treat you right")* from the learner's own point of view. All other responses were less than accurate. They subtracted from the learner's expression. Response 2 was incomplete because it responded only to feeling (level 2.5). Response 3, while it attended to the content, did not respond to feeling (level 2.0). Response 1 missed the mark in attempting to provide guidance to the learner (level 1.5). Response 5 was a good guidance response, indicating that the teacher attended to the content without being explicit about the feeling (level 2.0). This will become more clear to you as you learn how to respond accurately to the feeling and meaning expressed by the learner. You now know something about responding. You need to learn a lot more.

RESPONDING TRAINING

LEARNING TO RESPOND
TO YOUR LEARNERS

Attending, observing and listening behaviors make responding behavior possible. And responding behavior makes it possible for the learner to explore where she or he is, both in relation to her/himself and in relation to the learning material being presented. Until you and Maria—or Sal or Sara or Sandy—share an awareness of how she feels about her assignment and why she feels that way, neither of you can make progress; your accurate response reflects your understanding and helps Maria to explore more fully. As you remember from your preliminary discrimination training, the minimally effective response that enables the learners to explore themselves was the level 3.0, or high-low response. Making level 3.0 responses will be the goal of our responsiveness training. These responses are high on responsiveness, or the communication of understanding; and low on initiative, or the communication of direction and guidance.

Such high-low responses are interchangeable with the learners' responses. They capture the feeling and the reason for the feeling that the learners have expressed. In other terms, the teacher has expressed essentially the same message that the learners have communicated to her. We can compare the teacher's response to the learners' responses and agree that they are essentially identical in terms of the experience expressed by the learners.

Responsive behavior, in turn, lays the base for effective initiative behavior by giving us the understanding we need to provide guidance and direction. Responding to the learners assures them that we know where they are. Initiating with the learners helps to point up where they want to go. The learners will be more open to the direction and guidance that we provide when they are certain that we understand where they are.

RESPONDING TO FEELING

The first step in responsiveness training is responding to feeling. Understanding how a person feels is the most important part of understanding where he is. In order to respond to feelings, we must do several things. First, we must know what a feeling word is. Feeling words refer directly to feelings like happy, sad or mad. Some words which are used as feeling words are not really appropriate. One example is *"rejected."* This tells us what **happened**, not how the person feels about it: that is, he could be mad or he could be sad. Sometimes you can use a word or phrase which describes a situation in a figurative sense, such as *"You feel like climbing the walls,"* which represents feeling bored or alone, even though the individual may be surrounded by people. In order to determine the appropriate feeling word, you must use all the attending behaviors which you have learned. You must attend fully to the learner; you must observe the learner's behavior, particularly his or her facial expressions which give us cues to feelings; you must listen to the learner's voice because his or her tone of voice will also give us cues to feelings. You must listen to the learner's words. Then you can ask how he or she feels about the experience he or she has related to you, using behavioral cues and words together to decide the appropriate word. It is most important that you initially suspend your own frame of reference. Ignore the apparent irrationality of Tomas' rage; don't linger over thoughts like *"he shouldn't feel that way."* The goal in the first stage of human relations is simply to understand what the learner is saying and how he or she feels about it.

REPEATING EXPRESSIONS VERBATIM

Now we will engage in a responding exercise. We will practice responding to feeling.

Paul is a student who has come to you in a time of need. He is quiet but he experiences his feelings strongly and is searching for understanding. Written below, you will find his expression to you. Read the expression once and then cover it and try to write it verbatim. Practice your attending skills as you go through the exercise.

"I don't want to leave this school and all my friends, but Mom says we got to move because of Dad's job."

Now repeat Paul's expression verbatim. If you were able to repeat the **exact words** that Paul expressed to you, then you can move on to the next stage of the exercise.

ASKING HOW THE EXPRESSION
MAKES YOU FEEL

Now we will see if we can determine a
feeling word that is appropriate to Paul's
expression. Repeat Paul's expression verbatim
once again. Now ask yourself, *"How does that
make me (as Paul) feel?"* In other words, how
would you feel if you were in Paul's situation?
Write down the one feeling word that captures Paul's experience. Check and make sure
that you do have a feeling word.

FORMULATING A FEELING WORD

Now we will formulate a response to Paul that captures his expressed feeling. In other words, we will begin to communicate with Paul. Repeat Paul's expression. Ask yourself how Paul feels in this situation. It may or may not be the same as you would have felt. This doesn't matter. Neither agreeing nor disagreeing with Paul will do any good. He doesn't need a teacher who feels the same way or a teacher who rejects his feeling—he needs a teacher who can understand him! Use what you know about Paul to decide whether the feeling is appropriate for him or not. Does he usually seem to experience his feelings intensely or mildly? Is he a large or small person? Does the strength of my feeling fit him? Now take a full 30 seconds to think about the feeling word you use. Make sure it is the best feeling word you can think of to show Paul that you understand the feeling he is having. It takes time to crawl under someone else's skin—particularly when you don't know the person well. You must take time to reflect on what has been said, the tone and the visual cues you have. Therefore, although it seems like an eternity, it is important to practice delaying 30 seconds before responding so you have time to review the cues. If you attend to the student during this process, he will know you are working for him and will be glad to wait. Your delay communicates respect because you care enough to work for him. Later when you know the student better, you can respond more quickly. The goal for now is to select a word that is interchangeable with the feeling and the intensity of the feeling implied or expressed by the learner.

CHECKING OUT YOUR FEELING WORD

Anytime you are not sure you have a feeling word or the word is not precise enough, it is often helpful to just keep asking yourself how the learners would feel about the first word that you came up with. For example, if the first word that you came up with is *"good"* or *"bad,"* you might ask yourself *"How would the learners feel about that word?"* Perhaps they would feel pleased with themselves in relation to *"good"* or disgusted with themselves in relation to *"bad."* If you ask the same question again, they might say that they are really flying high, that they are happy with themselves and optimistic about their future in relation to the pleased feeling, or really feeling low and down on themselves and depressed about their future in relation to the disgusted feeling.

USING THE REFLECTIVE FORMAT

Now we will formulate a response directly to Paul. We will use the reflective format, *"You feel_____."* This format provides a structure which insures delivery. You can check yourself out to determine whether, in fact, you have delivered an accurate response to the student's experience. You can do a lot of good teaching with this format, even though it may seem stereotyped. Master the skills before you work on individualizing your presentation! Now let us use the reflective format to formulate a response to Paul's expression. Possible words that would have captured Paul's expressed feeling are *"sad,"* *"bad,"* *"scared"* or similar words. Whether you choose to use *"sad"* or *"scared"* depends on whether you think a student like Paul would own up to being scared. Remember, always keep in mind that you want to formulate responses that the learners can use.

USING FEELING WORDS

Now let us get some practice in responding to feeling. In order to capture a person's unique feeling experience, you will need a large repertoire of feeling words. On the following pages, you will find a list of feeling words. They are divided into categories of happy, sad, angry, confused, scared, weak and strong. These are categories that learners will use most often. Before practicing responding to feeling, try to add five words to each category which you could use with your learners. They may be slang terms. The important thing is that they are useful to the learners. Highly intellectual words are not as effective. Your words should reach for the gut experience and be understandable to the learners to whom you are responding. Study the word list before responding. Do not use the word list to fill in the blank feeling. You will be much more actively involved in learning to respond if you try to recall the words rather than passively reading.

LEARNING FEELING WORDS

On the following page is a list of words that describe human feelings. The feeling categories are not exhaustive but they do cover most human feelings. You may wish to add to the list. You may feel that some words belong in different categories. Put them wherever they fit for you. The important thing is to have them at your command. The critical test is the ability to communicate with the other person. You may wish to rank-order any words you add in terms of their level of intensity within each feeling category: strong, mild or weak.

Happy

aglow, alive, amused, anxious, blissful, bubbly, calm, cheerful, compassion, content, delighted, ecstatic, elated, enthralled, excited, exuberant, feel good, felicitous, fine, fortunate, full of life, gay, giddy, glad, gleeful, good, great, joyful, joyous, jubilant, lighthearted, love, lucky, marvelous, memorable, merry, motherly, overjoyed, peaceful, pleasant, pleased, proud, relieved, satisfied, smiley, thankful, thrilled, tranquil, turned on, up, uplifted, wonderful

Sad

angry, apathetic, bad, blue, burdened, crushed, deflated, dejected, despairing, despondent, depressed, disappointed, disenchanted, distressed, disturbed, down, downcast, downhearted, downtrodden, drab, dreary, dull, embarrassed, emotional, feeling unwanted, forlorn, gloomy, glum, grave, grieved, hate, heavy-hearted, hopeless, hurt, lonely, lost, low, low spirits, melancholy, miserable, mistrustful, moody, morose, mournful, negative, painful, pitiful, plaintive, remorseful, self-pitying, sober, somber, sorrowful, sorry, terrible, turned off, uneasy, unhappy, unloved, unpleasant, unwanted, upset, woeful

Angry

aggravated, agitated, anguished, annoyed, blustery, burned up, critical, cross, cutting, disgruntled, disgusted, dismayed, displeased, distraught, distressed, disturbed, enraged, exasperated, fed up, fierce, fiery, frantic, frenzied, frustrated, furious, hateful, hostile, hot-tempered, in a stew, incensed, indignant, inflamed, infuriated, intense, irate, irked, irritated, livid, mad, madness, mean, miffed, outraged, perturbed, provoked, rage, raving, revengeful, riled, seething, sore, spiteful, stormy, temper, troubled, uncontrollable, unrestrained

Confused

abashed, addled, anxious, baffled, befuddled, bewildered, bothered, chaotic, confounded, crazy, dazed, depressed, deranged, disconcerted, dismayed, disordered, disorganized, disoriented, distracted, distraught, disturbed, doubtful, embarrassed, flabbergasted, flustered, foggy, forgetful, frustrated, helpless, helter skelter, hopeless, jumbled together, left out, lost, mazed, mistaken, misunderstood, mixed up, muddled, nonplussed, obscure, out-of-it, panicky, perplexed, puzzled, scatterbrained, surprised, trapped, troubled, uncertain, uncomfortable, uncomposed, undecided, unsettled, unsure, untogether, upset, vague, weak

Scared

affrighted, afraid, aghast, alarmed, anxious, appalled, apprehensive, awed, chicken, confused, daunted, displeasure, distrustful, dreadful, fearful, frightened, harassed, horrified, insecure, intimidated, jumpy, leery, lonely, meek, nervous, panic-stricken, panicky, petrified, rattled, shaky, shy, spooked, startled, stunned, terrified, terrorized, threatened, timid, timorous, tormented, tremulous, uneasy, unpleasant, unstrung, unsure, worried

Weak

confused, deathly, deflated, defective, defenseless, deficient, delicate, disabled, dull, exhausted, exposed, feeble, fragile, frail, frustrated, gentle, helpless, ill, impotent, inadequate, incapable, inconsistent, ineffective, inferior, insecure, irresolute, lacking, laid low, languid, lethargic, lifeless, lost, meager, mild, pale, passive, powerless, puny, quiet, retiring, run-down, shaky, sickly, soft, spineless, stale, submissive, subtle, timid, unable, unable to cope, unconvincing, undernourished, unfit, unhinged, unsound, unstable, unsure, useless, vulnerable, wavering, wishy-washy, wobbly, worn out

Strong

able, active, adequate, aggressive, angry, assured, bold, brave, capable, confident, consistent, courageous, determined, durable, enduring, energetic, everlasting, fierce, firm, forceful, formidable, full of spirit, glorious, happy to be me, hardy, hate, healthy, herculean, impregnable, independent, indestructible, intense, invincible, loud, love, mean, mighty, muscular, opinionated, overwhelming, penetrating, positive, potent, powerful, productive, quick, rage, reliable, resistant, robust, secure, solid, stalwart, staunch, stout, super, surviving, vibrant, violent, well-being, zealous

BREAKING DOWN HAPPY FEELINGS

Here is a way that happy feelings may be broken down according to their level of intensity. They may be broken down into **strong**, **mild** and **weak** feeling words.

Feeling Category

Happy

Levels of Intensity

Strong			
	bubbly	excited	joyous
	delighted	exuberant	jubilant
	ecstatic	full of life	love
	elated	gleeful	marvelous
	enthralled	joyful	overjoyed
			thrilled

Mild			
	aglow	cheerful	proud
	alive	felicitous	relieved
	amused	gay	turned on
	anxious	giddy	up
	blissful	great	uplifted
		happy	wonderful

Weak			
	calm	glad	peaceful
	compassionate	good	pleasant
	content	lighthearted	pleased
	feel good	lucky	satisfied
	fine	memorable	smiley
	fortunate	motherly	thankful
			tranquil

BREAKING DOWN SAD FEELINGS

You may have put some of the words in different categories. Fine! Just be sure they communicate to the learners the feeling that they are expressing. Here are sad feelings at different levels of intensity.

Feeling Category

Sad

Levels of Intensity

Strong			
	burdened	distressed	morose
	crushed	downtrodden	mournful
	dejected	grave	remorseful
	despairing	grieved	sorrowful
	despondent	hopeless	terrible
	depressed	miserable	unloved
			unwanted

Mild			
	blue	forlorn	melancholy
	disappointed	gloomy	moody
	disturbed	heavy-hearted	pitiful
	downcast	hurt	plaintive
	downhearted	lonely	self-pitying
	feeling unwanted	low	upset
			woeful

Weak			
	angry	embarrassed	painful
	apathetic	emotional	sober
	bad	glum	sorry
	deflated	hateful	turned off
	disenchanted	lost	uneasy
	down	low spirits	unhappy
	drab	mistrustful	unpleasant
	dreary		

BREAKING DOWN ANGRY FEELINGS

You may have better words for the different levels of intensity. If so, add them. They will increase your response repertoire in the feeling areas involved. Here are angry feelings at different levels of intensity.

Feeling Category

Angry

Levels of Intensity

Strong	blowing up	hot-tempered	revengeful
	burned up	incensed	seething
	burning	indignant	spiteful
	cutting	infuriated	stormy
	enraged	intense	uncontrollable
	fierce	irate	unrestrained
	fiery	livid	violent
	frenzied	mad	wild
	furious	rage	wrathful
	hateful	raving	

Mild	acrimonious	fed up	miffed
	aggravated	frustrated	outraged
	agitated	hostile	perturbed
	anguished	hot	provoked
	annoyed	irked	riled
	disgusted	irritated	sore
	distressed	madness	upset
	exasperated	mean	

Weak	blustery	distraught	put out
	critical	disturbed	temper
	cross	frantic	troubled
	disgruntled	ill-humored	uptight
	dismayed	in a stew	wounded
	displeasure	inflamed	

102

BREAKING DOWN CONFUSED FEELINGS

You may find it helpful to keep an up-dated list of feeling words at different levels of intensity. Language changes over time. So, too, your understanding of words should broaden and deepen over time. Here are confused feelings at different levels of intensity.

Feeling Category

Confused

Levels of Intensity

Strong			
	abashed	dazed	jumbled together
	addled	deranged	mazed
	anxious	disconcerted	nonplussed
	befuddled	flabbergasted	perplexed
	bewildered	flustered	trapped
	chaotic	frustrated	troubled
	confounded	helter skelter	

Mild			
	baffled	foggy	out-of-it
	disordered	hopeless	panicky
	disorganized	left out	puzzled
	disoriented	misunderstood	scatterbrained
	distraught	mixed-up	uncomposed
	disturbed	muddled	upset
	doubtful	obscure	

Weak			
	bothered	forgetful	uncomfortable
	crazy	helpless	undecided
	depressed	lost	unsettled
	dismayed	mistaken	unsure
	distracted	surprised	untogether
	embarrassed	uncertain	vague
			weak

BREAKING DOWN SCARED FEELINGS

Just as you review your lesson plans, you will want to review your feeling word lists. This will keep your quantity of responses large. Here are scared feelings at different levels of intensity.

Feeling Category

Scared

Levels of Intensity

Strong	affrighted	appalled	panicky
	afraid	fearful	panic-stricken
	aghast	frightened	petrified
	alarmed	horrified	terrified
	anxious	intimidated	terrorized
			tormented
Mild	abashed	jumpy	threatened
	apprehensive	rattled	timorous
	chicken	shaky	uneasy
	daunted	spooked	unstrung
	harassed	startled	worried
	insecure	stunned	
Weak	confused	leery	shy
	displeasure	lonely	timid
	distrustful	meek	tremulous
	dreadful	nervous	unpleasant
			unsure

BREAKING DOWN WEAK FEELINGS

Your quantity of responses will, in turn, affect the quality of your responses. And the quality of your responses is what makes you effective. Here are feelings of weakness at different levels of intensity.

Levels of Intensity

Strong			
	debilitated	frail	languid
	decrepit	helpless	lethargic
	deficient	impotent	lifeless
	exhausted	infirm	marrowless
	exposed	insecure	puny
	faint	insipid	rickety
	feeble	irresolute	susceptible
	fragile	laid low	vulnerable

Mild			
	anemic	mild	unable
	deathly	pale	unfit
	defeated	passive	unforceful
	defenseless	powerless	unsound
	delicate	retiring	unstable
	easily led	run-down	unsure
	incapable	sickly	useless
	ineffective	spineless	wishy-washy
	inferior	stale	wobbly
	lacking		

Weak			
	confused	listless	submissive
	defective	lost	subtle
	disabled	meager	timid
	dull	meek	tired
	frustrated	negative	unconvincing
	gentle	not together	undernourished
	ill	quiet	unhinged
	inconsistent	shaky	vacillating
	inadequate	soft	wavering
			worn out

BREAKING DOWN STRONG FEELINGS

Remember, just as with your teaching subject matter, you cannot be spontaneous and creative in your responses if you do not have the basic responses in your repertoire in the first place. You can't convince Bill that you really understand how he feels unless you have a word or phrase that he can recognize as interchangeable with his original expression of being "super together!" This is the basic principle of teaching. This is the basic principle of communicating. Here are feelings of strength at different levels of intensity.

Feeling Category

Strong

Levels of Intensity

Strong	confident	herculean	mighty
	everlasting	impregnable	potent
	formidable	indestructive	powerful
	full of spirit	intense	secure
	happy to be me	invincible	stalwart
	hate	love	

Mild	aggressive	hardy	strapping
	bold	overwhelming	sturdy
	determined	penetrating	sure
	durable	resistant	tenacious
	energetic	robust	tough
	fierce	solid	unyielding
	firm	staunch	vigorous
	forceful	stout	

Weak	able	glorious	quick
	active	healthy	rage
	adequate	impact	reliable
	angry	independent	super
	assured	loud	surviving
	brave	mean	vibrant
	capable	muscular	violent
	consistent	opinionated	well being
	courageous	positive	zealous
	enduring	productive	

DISCRIMINATING FEELING CATEGORIES

By breaking the feelings into different categories, you facilitate the appropriateness of your response. When you have feeling words available to you in different categories, you can match the category with the feeling expressed by the learners. Thus, your feeling category question would be: *"Are they expressing happiness, sadness, anger, confusion, fear, weakness or strength?"* Your answer will put your feeling words in the appropriate feeling category.

Categories of Feelings

Happy   Sad   Angry   Scared   Confused   Weak   Strong

DISCRIMINATING LEVELS OF INTENSITY

By breaking down the feelings into different levels of intensity, you facilitate the accuracy of your response. When you have feeling words available to you at different levels of intensity, you can discriminate the precise level of intensity to match the learners' expression. Thus you can ask yourself: *"Are they expressing the feeling category at a high, moderate or low level of intensity?"* Your answer will put your feeling word at an accurate level of intensity.

Categories of Feelings

	Happy	Sad	Angry	Scared	Confused	Weak	Strong

Levels of Intensity   Strong

Mild

Weak

DISCRIMINATING FEELING CATEGORIES AND INTENSITY LEVELS

Over time, you will strive for increasingly appropriate and accurate feeling responses. You may do this by continuing to break feelings into subcategories and sublevels of intensity within categories. Thus, for example, within the strong intensity level of the happy category, you may develop different meaning categories and intensity levels.

These are very difficult exercises. They will stretch your awareness of feeling words. You cannot develop your word resources enough. You are only as free as your response repertoire. If your response repertoire is limited, you will make crude discriminations and, thus, rough and approximate responses. If your response repertoire is extensive, you will make fine discriminations and, thus, precise responses.

		Feeling Category	
		Happy	
Levels of Intensity		**Subcategories**	
Strong	Excited	Joy	Life
Sublevels of Intensity			
Strong	thrilled	ecstatic overjoyed	full of life love
Mild	excited	exuberant gleeful jubilant	enthralled
Weak	elated	delighted gleeful joyful joyous	bubbly

PRACTICING FEELING WORDS

Now let us practice formulating our responses using the reflective format *"You feel _____."* As you respond to each of the stimulus expressions below, practice attending and listening by making sure you know what has been said. Repeat it silently to yourself without looking. Delay at least 30 seconds to think of a feeling word. Here are some steps for thinking of a feeling word.

First, using verbal and nonverbal cues, decide on a broad category of feeling: that is, happy, sad, angry, confused, scared, strong or weak.

Second, review those words listed under these categories.

Third, decide on the accurate intensity of the feeling: strong, moderate or weak.

Fourth, recall a word which meets these requirements. If more than one feeling has been expressed, pick the more important feeling. If two feelings have been expressed equally, then you need two words.

Fifth, make sure it is a feeling word and make sure it is a word that the learners can use.

Now you are ready for the learners' expressions.

FORMULATING RESPONSES
TO FEELING

Learner Expression 1

"I've tried and tried to make friends since coming here, but still nobody likes me."

Formulate your response to the learner's expression of this feeling.

"You feel _____."

Learner Expression 2

"I get tired of school and can't see much use for it. And then I get to wondering just what would happen if I quit. There just has to be more to life than this, but I don't know what it is."

Formulate your response to the learner's expression of this feeling.

"You feel _____."

Learner Expression 3

"I just hate the kids. They're always doing mean and stupid things."

Formulate your response to the learner's expression of this feeling.

"You feel _____."

Learner Expression 4

"Hey! Guess what! I got elected. I can't believe it, but I did!"

Formulate your response to the feeling expressed by the learner.

"You feel _____."

Learner Expression 5

"I got the best grade of anybody in gym today on the fitness test. I worked and worked and then I was the best!"

Formulate your response to the feeling expressed by the learner.

"You feel _____."

Learner Expression 6

"That bus is really awful. There's so much tension on it. White kids in one group and black kids in another are always yelling at each other and picking fights. I just know it's going to explode."

Formulate your response to the feeling expressed by the learner.

"You feel _____."

Learner Expression 7

"I must be the dumbest kid you ever had. I try but I always do lousy. Maybe I should just quit."

Formulate your response to the feeling expressed by the learner.

"You feel _____."

Learner Expression 8

"I just love being in your class. You're the best teacher I ever had."

Formulate your response to the feeling expressed by the learner.

"You feel _____."

Learner Expression 9

"What the heck is going on? You keep giving us this stupid busy work. It's not relevant to anything. It's just a big waste of time."

Formulate your response to the feeling expressed by the learner.

"You feel _____."

Learner Expression 10

"Gee, I'm really disappointed. I was really looking forward to being in your class, but it just hasn't worked out. I really thought I would learn a lot, but I just haven't."

Formulate your response to the feeling expressed by the learner.

"You feel _____."

Now you should look over your responses. The feelings which you have formulated should match up with the feelings expressed by the learners. If they do not, go back over your word list and select a more appropriate feeling word to respond to the learners.

Sample Responses

Learner Expression	Category of Feeling	Intensity of Feeling	Accurate & Interchangeable Response
No. 1	sad	mild/strong	lonely/miserable
No. 2	confused	mild	mixed-up
No. 3	angry	strong	mad
No. 4	happy	strong	thrilled
No. 5	strong	mild	proud
No. 6	scared	strong	afraid
No. 7	weak	mild	down
No. 8	happy	mild	happy
No. 9	angry	mild	fed up
No. 10	sad	mild	letdown

These are by no means the only possible responses. Remember, the test question is *"Would the learner see my feeling word as an accurate reflection of her or his real feeling?"*

112

RESPONDING TO FEELING
IN THE CLASSROOM

Now practice responding to feeling for a large group of learners in the classroom. Try to identify the feelings they are expressing by asking yourself how would their experiences make you feel. At a minimum, make gross discriminations about whether your groups of learners or the entire class are feeling *"up"* or *"down."* Then respond to them using feeling words that reflect their *"good"* or *"bad"* feelings. A gang of boys in one corner, supposedly working on a group project, are laughing and talking excitedly. You might respond *"Well, you guys sure feel full of life today!"* By responding accurately, you can account for the important feeling dimensions of your entire group of learners' learning experience. And you will prepare the group for exploring the meaning or reason for the feeling.

RESPONDING TO MEANING

RESPONDING TO FEELING AND MEANING

Responding to how the person feels is critical but it is also incomplete. To communicate a complete understanding of what the learners are saying, you also have to recognize the meaning of their statements. Meaning is the reason for the feeling. Meaning is a combination of the feeling and the content. When responding to the meaning, do not simply repeat the content of what the learners have said; rather, try to capture and express the personal reason for the feeling. Let us look at the following illustration of an expression by an elementary school child.

"They're always picking on me! You know, ganging up on me and pushing me around. I don't even want to go to school anymore."

Here the teacher's response might be as follows:

"You feel scared because they might really hurt you."

The *"might really hurt you"* part of the teacher's response supplies the learner's reason for the feeling. It summarizes the meaning in a personal way rather than just repeating the content.

LEARNING THE REASON FOR THE FEELING

Responding to meaning, then, is simply providing the reason for the feeling. Here are several more illustrations that might help you learn this skill.

"You feel sad because the teacher didn't pick you."

"You feel angry because the teacher didn't even think about you."

"You feel happy because the teacher made you captain of the team."

Each of these three illustrations relates to the teaching situation. In each illustration, the reason for the feeling (the meaning) is used to complement the feeling response.

COMPLEMENTING THE
FEELING WITH MEANING

Now let us go back and formulate a complete feeling and meaning response to Paul. Use the format *"You feel_____ because_____."* The *"you feel"* part captures the feeling. The *"because"* part supplies the reason for the feeling. For example, Paul's problem was expressed as follows:

"I don't want to leave this school and all my friends, but Mom says we got to move because of Dad's job."

Write down your response to the feeling expressed by Paul. It may be the same response which you made before. *"You feel_____."* Give the meaning or reason for the feeling using the format *"You feel_____ because_____."*

A possible response to Paul might be as follows:

"You feel sad, because all the people you like will be left behind."

PRACTICING FEELING AND MEANING RESPONSES

You have now learned to formulate high responsive-low initiative or level 3.0 responses. You can respond accurately to the learners and thus facilitate their exploration of where they are. These interchangeable responses are termed *"minimally effective"* interpersonal responses because, at a minimum, the teacher is able to communicate her understanding of the learners to the learners. When you think about it, that's really not too much to expect: to be at least able to understand the learners at the level at which they have presented themselves; to be able to recognize young Brad's problem, for example, by attending to him physically, observing his tear-streaked face and woeful expression, listening to his words and tone of voice; and to be able to respond to him accurately and fully by using a vocabulary of feeling terms that he can recognize. Indeed, there can be no effective teaching without this minimally effective response!

PRACTICING RESPONDING TO YOUR LEARNERS' EXPRESSIONS

Now we will practice responding to feeling and meaning in the classroom. First pick out the children with whom you think you have a very good relationship. By starting with the learners with whom you have the best relationship, you build in success for yourself and for them. Leave the learners whom you are having difficulty reaching until later. This way you will have more mastery of the skills when you come to them. In general, move from the learners with whom you have the best relationship to those with whom you have the poorest relationship. Next, find or create an opportunity to respond to the learners using the format *"You feel_____ because _____."* Do not forget your attending, observing and listening skills. Be sure to note their reactions to your response. They should go on to talk more about where they are in relation to themselves, to you or to the learning material. In some way, they should acknowledge that you have reached them.

RESPONDING ON A REGULAR BASIS

Next, we will increase the number of students whom you will reach. Increase by one per day the number of learners you are responding to until you are responding to at least 15 to 20 different learners each day. As you start to build a number of responses each day, you may want to begin to vary the format. Here are some alternatives: *"It feels _____ when _____."* Or, *"You're feeling _____ when _____."* Or *"You feel like _____ because _____."* Do not use *"You feel* **that** *_____."* This format always leaves out the feeling word because it tends to emphasize meaning.

Now respond to each learner you have in cycles of 15 to 20. If you have 30 students, each learner should be responded to at an average of every other day. If you have 150 students, each learner should receive a response at least once every 10 days. Evidence indicates that this responsiveness alone will make a significant difference in the responsive atmosphere of your classroom and thus in the achievement and growth of your learners.

RESPONDING IN THE CLASSROOM

Now practice responding to both feeling and meaning for a large group of learners in the classroom. You have made gross discriminations about whether the class or groups of learners are feeling *"good"* or *"bad."* Now identify the reason for these feelings. For example, your learners may be feeling positive and optimistic because they all passed a recent test with flying colors. In such a situation, of course, the reason for their collective *"up"* feeling is their excellent performance. Here you might respond to feeling and meaning with a statement like *"You all feel glad because the test turned out to be so easy!"* You can communicate your understanding to your entire group of learners in your feeling and meaning response.

PRACTICING RESPONDING
IN THE CLASSROOM

Now put your responses to feeling and meaning together by responding fully in the classroom. Again, try to repeat verbatim or repeat the gist of the expressions that the learners have made. With groups of learners, you may want to attempt to categorize the topics or the content of the expression. For example, in relation to the learning tasks, do the expressions have to do with subjects, activities or materials? Look for any common themes that you might hear, especially those that are repeated by different learners or different groups of learners. Then identify the feelings and the reason for the feelings and communicate your understanding to your entire group of learners. That way your learners will be able to explore where they are in relation to the learning tasks. And you will eventually be able to personalize their understanding of their explorations.

PRACTICING MAKING APPLICATIONS
IN THE CLASSROOM

Again, see if you can apply two or more translations of responding in the classroom. Consider the interactions between learners as well as between you and the learners. Now practice responding to feeling and meaning on a regular basis. Try to make sure that you respond accurately to each learner at least once every week or two. Many children have never had their experiences responded to accurately in their entire lifetimes. The principle of reciprocal effect will work for you in facilitating the learners' responsiveness to you and your teaching efforts. Indeed, later on you may want to teach them directly how to respond in learning.

POST-TRAINING
RESPONDING ASSESSMENT

USING YOUR RESPONDING SKILLS

Now let us make a post-training assessment of your responding skills. We will ask you once again to respond as accurately as you can to the learner's experience at the level at which he or she has expressed it. Write your response exactly as you would say it to the student. Do not describe what you would talk about. In the following exercise, a learner expresses the following concern.

"I don't know. Nothing ever works out right. I guess I'm just going to leave school when I get old enough."

Please formulate the most accurate response that you can make to the expression.

Your response.

DISCRIMINATING ACCURATE RESPONDING

Let us read again the learner's expression. Then let us read the five alternative teacher responses. We will ask you to rate these responses from 1.0 (very ineffective) to 5.0 (extremely effective) with 3.0 being the minimally effective response which reflects most accurately the student's experience. You can assign equal ratings to different responses if you consider them to be equally effective in capturing the feeling and the reason for this feeling. Split the gaps between levels as much as is appropriate.

"I don't know. Nothing ever works out right. I guess I'm just going to quit school when I get old enough."

Your Rating

————1. *"You feel disappointed."*

————2. *"You better stay in school or you'll never get anywhere."*

————3. *"You feel disappointed because nothing seems to work for you in school."*

————4. *"You should explore what you can do in and out of school before you quit."*

————5. *"You feel sad because everything's going badly."*

CHECKING OUT YOUR DISCRIMINATIONS

The trained raters' ratings are listed in the table below. You may determine your discrimination score by obtaining the absolute deviations, adding them and dividing the total by 5. The result is your responding discrimination score.

Teacher Responses	Ratings	Your Ratings	Difference (Deviations)
1	2.5	− _____	= _____
2	1.5	− _____	= _____
3	3.0	− _____	= _____
4	2.0	− _____	= _____
5	3.0	− _____	= _____

Total = _____ = _____
$$\frac{\quad}{5}$$

Responding Discrimination Score

RECEIVING FEEDBACK

Additional feedback on your ratings will help to reinforce your learnings about attending. Ratings of level 3.0 mean that the teacher has responded interchangeably to both the feeling and meaning expressed by the learners. Both rated at level 3.0, responses 3 and 5 are the models for minimally effective levels of responding. Less than this is less than is necessary to help. Accordingly, responding to feeling alone is rated at level 2.5 (Response 1). Responding to content is rated at level 2.0 (Response 4). Poor guidance response is rated at level 1.5 (Response 2).

UNDERSTANDING RESPONDING

You should have improved in your discrimination of accurate responding. The rating of level 3.0 was assigned to the third and fifth teacher responses because they both reflected accurately and interchangeably the feeling and meaning expressed by the learner. The first response captured only the feeling. The fourth response was a good guidance response although it captured only the content. The second response again missed the mark in providing guidance. If your discrimination has not improved or if it deviates more than one-half level from the trained raters, then you should reread the chapter. If your discrimination score deviates less than one-half level, then you are eligible to rate your level of responding on the pre- and post-responding tests. Once again, you could develop your own scale for responding. Your rating of your responding should have improved significantly from before to after responding training. You are now ready to respond accurately to your learners.

Level 1.0—No expression or expression unrelated to student
Level 1.5—Expression related to student—usually poor guidance
Level 2.0—Responding to content—usually some guidance
Level 2.5—Responding to feeling
Level 3.0—Responding to feeling and meaning interchangeably

Responding Skills

Pre-Training   **Post-Training**

———Your Rating   ———Your Rating

MASTERING RESPONDING

Once you have mastered responding skills, you have taken another step toward effective teaching. Teachers who attend and respond are minimally effective at level 3.0. You are equipped to respond to where your learners are. Your learners know that you have heard what they said. When Angelo swears, your responding skills are the first step you can take toward changing his verbal behavior. *"You feel angry because you didn't do it right, Angelo."* Your response tells Angelo that you have heard him swear and that you know how he feels and why. When Karen says that she does not know which number to divide by, you will respond, *"You feel frustrated because you don't know where to begin."* You will continue to respond to Karen while you and she explore just what she does not understand. Then Karen will know that you are trying to identify what her learning problem is.

Mastery of responding behaviors insures that you will be ready to solve discipline problems. You will identify your learners' feelings and when you respond, your learners will explore themselves. When Angelo begins to understand that he swears when he does not do well, he is ready for the next step. Your responding skills help you diagnose the students' learning problems. Responding enables you to help your learners explore. Exploration helps your learners begin to understand themselves.

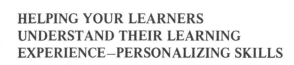

EXPERIENCING PERSONALIZING

The black boy raised his hand in response to the teacher's question about the justice system. *"Everytime you see cops, there's trouble,"* he offered. *"I understand,"* she answered, *"that's because the police are called in response to trouble."* *"No,"* he thought to himself, *"it seems to me they're always causing the trouble."* The boy looked at the teacher, trying to figure out a way to help her to understand what he was really saying. He thought out loud: *"You know, I'm really not sure teachers can help me live on the streets of my community!"* *"I understand,"* the teacher replied, *"but you must stay in school or you will not have the respect of the other citizens in your community."* *"I understand,"* he mused, *"means I do not."*

LEARNING PERSONALIZING SKILLS

You learn to personalize so that you can understand your learners—and so you can help them take control of their own lives and problems. In this context, personalizing to understand simply means that the teacher uses her own experience to help the learners to determine where they are in relation to where they want to go. Without an understanding of where they want to go, no goals may be developed. Without an understanding of where they want to go, no effective action program to achieve the goals is possible. Teacher personalizing facilitates the learners' understanding of where they are in relation to where they want to be. Before we begin the understanding module, let us check out the level of your personalizing skills.

Teacher: **Helping Skills**   Attending ▶ Responding ▶ Personalizing

Students: **Learning Skills**   Exploring   Understanding

126

PRE-TRAINING
PERSONALIZING ASSESSMENT

FORMULATING PERSONALIZED
RESPONSES

With good teacher responses, the learners can often explore where they are in relation to a great many things. But they may have difficulty understanding where they are in relation to where they want to be. It is the teacher's task to respond to the learners at the level that they express themselves in order to help them explore where they are. This lays the base for understanding the learners at levels that they do not express explicitly. The source of the teacher's understanding is the learners' deficit behavior or, in other terms, the gap between where they are and where they want to be. We will now ask you to respond to a learner expression. In responding, please formulate in writing the response that communicates the greatest understanding of where the learners are in relation to where they want to be. Write your response exactly as you would say it to the learner. Do not describe what you would talk about. In the following exercise, a student comes to you and expresses the following concern.

"I've been working real hard, but the stuff that has reading in it is holding me back."

Please formulate the most helpful understanding response that you can to the learner's expression.

Your response: _____

_____

_____

_____

_____

_____

DISCRIMINATING PERSONALIZED RESPONSES

Sometimes it's pretty frustrating to get it down on paper. You know you have a *"feel"* for what you want to say but somehow you just cannot say it the way you want to. You may also realize how important it is to be able not only to grasp but to communicate your understanding. If you do not do so effectively, your learners may end up working on goals that are wrong for them.

Now let us read once again the expression of this student after which we will read five alternative teacher responses. Please rate the responses from 1.0 to 5.0 with level 4.0 reflecting the response that most effectively communicates an understanding of where the learner is and where she wants to be. Split the gaps between levels where it is appropriate.

"I've been working real hard but the stuff that has reading in it is holding me back."

Your Rating

_____ 1. *"You feel real bad because the reading is real hard."*

_____ 2. *"You're disappointed because you aren't moving ahead very fast."*

_____ 3. *"You're sad because things just aren't working out."*

_____ 4. *"You're sad because you just haven't been able to handle things."*

_____ 5. *"You feel real bad because you haven't been able to handle the reading and you want to be able to handle it."*

128

CHECKING OUT YOUR PERSONALIZED DISCRIMINATIONS

Trained raters who have demonstrated the validity of their ratings in studies of helping and teaching outcome rated each of the teacher's attempts to communicate understanding of the learner's experience. These ratings are listed in the table below. You may determine your discrimination score by obtaining your absolute deviations, adding them and dividing the total by 5. The result is your discrimination score.

Teacher Responses	Ratings	Your Ratings	Difference (Deviations)
1	3.0	− _____	= _____
2	3.5	− _____	= _____
3	3.0	− _____	= _____
4	3.5	− _____	= _____
5	4.0	− _____	= _____

$$\text{Total} = \frac{\rule{2cm}{0.4pt}}{5} = \rule{2cm}{0.4pt}$$

Personalizing Understanding Discrimination Score

LEARNING ABOUT PERSONALIZING UNDERSTANDING

An exploration of the ratings will serve to prepare you for the training module. The key to a personalized response is its inclusion of a specific learner problem which is causing his or her present feeling—and its simultaneous reflection of where the learner wants to be. The rating of level 4.0 was assigned to response 5 because it personalized both where the learner was *("You haven't been able to handle the reading.")* and where she wanted to be *("You want to be able to handle it.")*. Ratings of level 3.0 were assigned to interchangeable responses 1 and 3. Ratings of level 3.5 were assigned to responses 2 and 4 because they personalized the response to the learner's expression by relating it to her rather than to some external force in the world. This will become more clear to you as you learn how to communicate understanding to the learners. You now know something about personalizing understanding. You need to learn a lot more.

PERSONALIZING SKILLS

PERSONALIZING UNDERSTANDING

Attending and responding make understanding possible. In the context of a responsive base, personalizing skills enable the teacher to help the learners to understand where they are in relation to where they want to go. As you remember from your preliminary discrimination training, the high responsive-high initiative response (High-High) was rated at level 4.0. Making level 4.0 responses will be our first goal in initiative training. We will call those teacher responses that help the learners to understand where they are in relation to where they want to be **additive understanding responses**. We call these responses additive understanding responses because they go beyond what the learners have expressed themselves. The responses add to their own understanding of themselves. Additive understanding responses, in turn, lay the base for developing programs to get the learners from where they are to where they want to be. Understanding where the learners want to be helps to establish the goal of the program. Understanding where the learners are helps to establish the first step in the program.

BUILDING AN
INTERCHANGEABLE BASE

LAYING A RESPONSIVE
BASE FOR INITIATING

In order to help the learners understand where they are in relation to where they want to be, you must first build a responsive base. The first step in moving toward higher levels of responsiveness involves building a base of understanding. You can do this best by facilitating the learners' exploration of where they are through the use of responses which are high on responsiveness and low on initiative: that is, the feeling and meaning responses which you have already learned to make. Let us return to Paul and help him to explore himself while at the same time coming to understand more clearly how he sees the world. Paul has said:

"I don't want to leave this school and all my friends, but Mom says we got to move because of Dad's job."

Your response: *"You feel_____*

because_____

_____"

As Paul continues, formulate responses in writing to him using the *"You feel_____ because_____"* format that captures the feeling and meaning of his expression.

Paul continues:

Paul: *"I've known these kids all my life. We've always lived here."*

Your response: *"You feel _____*

because_____

_____"

Paul: *"I've never had to make friends before and I don't know if I can do it."*

Your response: *"You feel _____*

because_____

_____"

Paul: *"I'm really going to be alone."*

Your response: *"You feel _____*

because_____

_____"

131

CHECKING OUT YOUR RESPONSIVE BASE

Here are some responses an effective teacher might have made to Paul.

Paul: *"I don't want to leave this school and all my friends but Mom says we got to move because of Dad's job."*

Teacher: *"You feel sad because all the people you like will be left behind."*

Paul: *"I've known these kids all my life. We've always been here."*

Teacher: *"You feel pretty worried because moving and meeting new kids will be a brand new experience for you."*

Paul: *"I'm really going to be alone."*

Teacher: *"You feel shook up because you think about being out there on your own."*

PRACTICING LAYING YOUR
RESPONSIVE BASE

You may wish to have some further practice in laying a responsive base. Mary is a high school girl having some difficulty in school. Respond to her in writing just as if you were talking to her.

Mary: *"I can't see why you gave me a C on my social studies paper. I worked at it a lot longer than some other kids who got A's."*

Your response:_____

_____

_____

Mary: *"Nobody cares how hard you work around here or anything."*

Your response:_____

_____

_____

Mary: *"Sometimes I think teachers have favorites and that's all that matters."*

Your response:_____

_____

_____

Mary: *"I also wonder what's wrong with me that I don't do better. It can't be all of them. Like, I really don't know what I did wrong on this paper. But it's not just this paper. It happens on other things too."*

Your response:_____

_____

_____

Mary: *"I really do want to do well. It's important to me."*

Your response:_____

_____

_____

Mary: *"But, I just don't know how to do better."*

Your response:_____

_____

_____

CHECKING OUT YOUR
RESPONSIVE BASE

You may wish to look again at some responses that an effective teacher might have made to Mary.

Mary: *"I can't see why you gave me a C on my social studies paper. I worked at it a lot longer than some other kids who got A's."*

Teacher: *"It really bugs you because I don't seem to appreciate your effort."*

Mary: *"Nobody ever cares how hard you work around here or anything."*

Teacher: *"You're furious because you don't think you really matter to me."*

Mary: *"Sometimes I think teachers just have their favorites and that's all that matters."*

Teacher: *"You're pretty bitter because you think I might be shortchanging you."*

Mary: *"I also wonder what's wrong with me that I didn't do better. It can't be all of them. Like, I really didn't know what I did wrong on this paper. But it's not just this paper. It happens in other things too."*

Teacher: *"You're pretty confused because you can't seem to figure out just what is expected of you."*

Mary: *"I really want to do well. It's important to me."*

Teacher: *"You're discouraged because sometimes you end up feeling small in your own eyes."*

Mary: *"But I don't know how to do better."*

Teacher: *"It's really frustrating for you because you can't make it pay off more for you."*

If your responses were similar to those made by the teacher to Mary, you have laid an effective base of understanding and you're ready to translate this understanding to classroom experience.

DEVELOPING YOUR RESPONSIVE BASE IN THE CLASSROOM

Now we will build a responsive base in class. Practice responding at an interchangeable level to learners for an extended period of time. As before, be sure to start with learners with whom you have a good relationship. Start by making two interchangeable responses and work your way up, one response at a time, to six or more responses. As you build the length of the interaction, it may be more appropriate to respond to learners outside the normal classroom interaction.

PERSONALIZING RESPONSES

PERSONALIZING YOUR RESPONSES

It is often difficult to do anything with expressions about third parties or situations. Learners often blame their parents or friends or teachers or some material like a test for their current predicament. And yet you may not be able to do anything about any of these other people or things. One course available to you is to personalize your response to the learners. By personalizing your response, we mean involving the learners directly in their expression of their experience. By personalizing your response, you make the learners responsible directly for the feeling and meaning which they have expressed. In this way, you help them assume control.

PERSONALIZING MEANING

Your personalized response should clearly pinpoint the learners' part in their own experience. You want to put the focus upon them. You want to make the learners responsible or accountable for their part in the experience. The format that you can use to do this most effectively is as follows: *"You feel _____ _____ because you _____ _____."*

The first step is to ask: given the experience which they have expressed, what are the implications for the learners? That is, what are the direct implications of their experience for the learners' behavior? The answer to this question will provide the personalized reason for the feeling.

Thus, in establishing an interchangeable base with Paul, the teacher might have formulated the following response to Paul's expression concerning his experience of having to leave his old home to move to a new home: *"You feel sad because all of the people you like will be left behind."*

In personalizing the meaning, the teacher must answer the question of the implications of the experience for Paul. Here it may become clear that Paul's experience revolves around his being alone. Accordingly, the teacher might formulate a response that incorporates this personalized meaning: *"You feel sad because you will be alone."*

PERSONALIZING THE PROBLEM

A further step in personalizing the meaning is to personalize the problem. You can personalize the problem by shifting the focus to what the learners are unable to do, i.e., where they have a behavioral deficit. In so doing, you may modify the format as follows: *"You feel_____ because you cannot_____."*

It is a simple step from personalizing the meaning to personalizing the problem. Thus, for Paul, the teacher personalized the meaning with the response, *"You feel sad because you will be alone."* Now, we express his being left alone in terms of a deficit in his repertoire of responses. In other words, he is being left alone because he is unable to make new friends in his new home. Accordingly, the teacher might formulate a response that incorporates the personalized problem: *"You feel sad because you will be alone and unable to make new friends in your new home."*

Sometimes, you will find yourself going directly to personalizing the problem. However, do so with care. Personalizing the meaning provides an intermediary step that makes the personalized problem more acceptable to the learners.

PERSONALIZING FEELING

You personalize the meaning by considering the implications of the experience for the learners' behavior. Now you will further personalize the feeling. You personalize the feeling by considering the implications for the learners' feelings of the personalized meaning response. Thus, for Paul, you personalized the meaning and the problem, *"because you will be alone and unable to make new friends in your new home."* Now you must ask the question: *"What are the implications for Paul's feelings of being alone and unable to make new friends?"* The answer will provide you with your personalized feeling response. Clearly, Paul is not sad about being alone. Paul is scared: *"You feel scared because you will be alone and unable to make new friends in your new home."* Personalizing the feeling and the meaning provides you with a means for going beyond what the learners have expressed. The techniques of personalizing allow you to search out new, deeper and more accurate feelings and meanings in responding to the learners.

PRACTICING PERSONALIZING

If you have no relationship or only a poor relationship with the learners, it might be preferable to respond quite a number of times at the interchangeable level (3.0). If you have a positive relationship with them, you might move to this more full involvement after only a few responses. Of course, if the learners are personalizing the material in their exploration, this is a clear signal to you that they are ready for you to respond in the fuller manner. Now let us practice once again responding to feeling and meaning about self.

First, go through your previous responses to Paul. Try to personalize the meaning and then the feeling. Change them to fit the *"You feel_____ because you (cannot) _____"* format. The feeling may or may not need to be changed.

Next, go through your previous responses to Mary. Personalize the meaning and the feeling. Change them to fit the *"You feel___ _____because you (cannot)_____ _____"* format. Look at the last two responses to Paul and the last three responses to Mary made by the effective teacher. These are some possible responses to feeling and meaning about self.

Now go back over the 10 exercises which you had in your early responsiveness training. Personalize the meaning and the feeling. Change them to fit the *"You feel_____ because you (cannot)_____"* format.

PERSONALIZING RESPONSES

Now let us practice more translations to the classroom. Begin to respond to the more personal feeling and meaning expressed by the learners with whom you have been able to respond accurately at an interchangeable level. Perhaps Andy has come to you to complain about the treatment another teacher has been giving him. And perhaps you've laid an effective base for personalizing by responding to his explicit feeling and meaning six or more times—responses along the lines of *"You feel furious because Mr. Smith seems to pick on you unfairly."* Now you might begin to respond at a more personalized level by saying *"You feel furious because you're the only person he treats like that."* This response personalizes the meaning which the situation has for Andy. You might then go on to personalize the problem in terms of a behavioral deficit and the new feeling (if any) which Andy's perception of this deficit may arouse.

Practice this with at least one learner a day. Extend the number of *"You feel_____ because you (cannot)_____"* responses you make in a row. If you can make six personalized responses with the feeling and meaning to each learner, then you are ready to learn additive skills. Remember, if the learners continue to explore new material, your responses have been interchangeable.

PERSONALIZING RESPONSES IN THE CLASSROOM

Now practice personalizing meaning, problems and feelings for a large group of learners in the classroom. Thus, for example, you may personalize the reason for the group's feeling by discriminating whether the learners got a step or item *"right"* or *"wrong."* Thus, the item was *"easy"* or *"hard"* because they got it *"right"* or *"wrong."* You may personalize the group's problem by discriminating whether the learners *"can"* or *"cannot"* do the step or item. Finally, you may personalize the group's feelings by discriminating whether the learners feel *"really good"* or *"really bad"* about their ability or inability to do the step or item. In this manner, you will prepare your group of learners for personalizing their goals.

PERSONALIZING UNDERSTANDING

ADDING TO THE
LEARNERS' UNDERSTANDING

Responsive skills have facilitated the learners' exploration of where they are in relation to themselves, to you and to the learning material. Now we are going to make personalized understanding responses in the context of a responsive base. Where the learners want to be can be understood most easily in terms of their personalized problem: the goal is the flip-side of the problem. You can understand where they want to be if you understand what deficits limit them to where they are. The goal here is for you to establish a direction which the learners can use within their frames of reference. You can do this by responding to the discrepancy between where the learners are and where they want to be, or need to be. The longer you explore the learners' concerns, the easier these steps will be.

First, think about where the learners are saying they are in their past few responses.

Second, think about any behaviors or capabilities that the learners lack.

Third, think about where the learners are saying they are in relation to where they want to be.

Fourth, think about what feeling they have about that goal.

Fifth, formulate a response as follows: *"You feel_____ because you (cannot)_____ and you want to _____ ."*

DISCRIMINATING PERSONALIZED UNDERSTANDING RESPONSES

While feeling continues to be important in these responses, personalized understanding usually emphasizes the meaning. It is the meaning which gives the direction and guidance to the learners. For example, here is a boy speaking to his teacher:

Learner: *"I didn't make the team."*

Teacher: *"You feel really discouraged because you didn't measure up and you want very much to measure up."*

The teacher responds to the boy's initial discouragement and the reason for it. This is where the student is. The teacher than supplies a direction by personalizing his understanding of the implied goal of catching up. All this is done from within the learner's frame of reference. Here is an illustration from a young girl:

Learner: *"Unless I can handle Math and I'm not doing it this year, I guess I'm never gonna be good at business."*

Teacher: *"You feel pretty disappointed because you just haven't been able to handle Math and you want to be a business person and this requires a good math background."*

Again, the teacher has responded to the learner's disappointment and the reason for this disappointment. But she has also personalized her response to the goal implied by the learner's expression. Here is a last example, an elementary school girl to the teacher:

Learner: *"Those kids keep calling me 'fatso' because I'm so big. Well, if they don't cut it out, they're gonna find out how big I am!"*

Teacher: *"You're angry with them and with yourself too because you let them make fun of your size and you want to stop them from treating you that way."*

Again, the teacher responds to where the learner is and where she wants to go.

PRACTICING MAKING PERSONALIZED UNDERSTANDING RESPONSES

Some of these responses involve fairly large leaps. You increase your chances of success and your chances of the learners being able to follow your initiative if you make the leaps smaller. You do this by laying the responsive base. Two people whom you know more about are Paul and Mary. You can practice establishing a direction with them. First, read over your interaction with Paul; then formulate a response to him that shows both personalized understanding and direction. Use the format *"You feel_____ because you (cannot)_____and you want to _____."* Repeat the same steps with Mary.

CHECKING OUT YOUR PERSONALIZED
UNDERSTANDING RESPONSES

Here is a personalized understanding response which an effective teacher might have made to Paul based on the responsive base which he had already established with Paul:

"Paul, you feel vulnerable because you don't know how to make friends and you want very much to be able to."

The teacher responds to Paul's feeling of vulnerability and the reason for it and directs Paul toward his implied goal of learning how to make friends. Here is another illustration of a personalized understanding response to Mary built upon the responsive base which the teacher has already constructed:

"You feel lost right now because you haven't been able to handle your school assignments and you want very much to be able to handle them."

These responses are both high in responsiveness and high in initiative. They communicate a personalized understanding of where the persons are and where they want to be. As you can see, the more of a responsive base you have, the easier it is to formulate personalized understanding responses. For further practice in making personalized responses, return to the 10 exercises which you have worked on previously. Focus on understanding where the learners are and directing them toward where they want to be.

PERSONALIZING YOUR LEARNERS' UNDERSTANDING IN CLASS

Let us make some translations toward responding with direction to learners in the classroom. Again, first pick the learners with whom you have been able to respond successfully in the past. You can respond to them again using both the *"You feel_____ because_____"* and the *"You feel _____ because you (cannot) _____"* format. This will give you the responsive base that you need. Now formulate a response that captures both where the learners are and where they want to be. Utilize the following format in doing so, *"You feel_____because you (cannot)_____and you want to_____."* Remember poor picked-upon Andy a few pages back. You might eventually respond to him by saying *"You feel miserable because you can't figure out how to get on Mr. Smith's good side and you really want him to act friendly toward you."* When you know that you can make personalized responses to your learners with some facility, then you are ready to get a further understanding of the exercises that you have completed.

PERSONALIZING UNDERSTANDING IN THE CLASSROOM

Now practice personalizing understanding for a large group of learners in the classroom. This might involve simply flipping over the personalized group problem to determine the personalized group goal. For example, if you have personalized the group problem *("cannot do")* you may personalize the group goal *("can do").*

PERSONALIZING FULLY

Now put your personalized responses to feeling, meaning, problems and goals together by personalizing fully in the classroom. This means identifying the feelings, the goals and the benefits to be accomplished.

You may personalize the group goal *("can do")* by attacking the benefits in terms of the personalized group feeling *("good")* and meaning *("getting it right")*. This will enable you to define the goal and the benefits to be achieved.

MAKING APPLICATIONS OF PERSONALIZING IN THE CLASSROOM

See if you can make several applications of personalizing in the classroom. Again, include the interactions between learners as well as between you and the learners. For example, you might personalize the understanding of a small group of learners who are unable to perform a particular skill but really want to be able to do so: *"You all feel bad because you can't figure out this material and you really want to get the assignment right."* Try to make sure that you personalize fully with each learner before the beginning of each new unit of learning. That way you will always be able to relate the learners' frames of reference to the learning goals. Later on, you may want to teach your learners directly how to personalize their own understanding in learning.

PRACTICING ALTERNATIVES
TO ADDITIVE RESPONSES

The personalized understanding response is the preferred response for helping the learners to understand where they are in relation to where they want to be. There are other possible ways of communicating this to the learners. Sometimes, the learners are unable to use the personalized response. If you have established a broad responsive base, you may choose to **confront** the learners. For example, if the learners consistently do not explore where they are effectively in a particular instance or deny where they need to go, you may choose to confront them with a discrepancy between (1) where they believe they are and where you believe they are; (2) where they believe they want to go and where you believe they need to go; (3) where they are and where you believe they need to be. Confrontations may take the simple format: *"On the one hand you believe_____ while on the other hand you appear to be_____ ."* A caution: confrontations are most effective in a responsive base. Indeed, if you have the time, you can achieve everything through additive understanding that you can through confronting—and more! Confrontations are only last resort measures dictated by time and resource limitations. Confrontation is never necessary and never sufficient. Yet, in the hands of a responsive teacher, it may be efficient.

POST-TRAINING
PERSONALIZING ASSESSMENT

USING YOUR PERSONALIZING SKILLS

Now let us make a post-training assessment of your personalizing understanding skills. We will ask you once again to understand the learners as fully as you can. This means communicating an understanding of where they are in relation to where they want to be. Write your response exactly as you would say it to the learners. Do not simply describe what you would talk about. In the following exercise, a young girl expresses her experience.

"I don't like it here. Why can't I go to school in my own neighborhood?"

Please formulate the most effective understanding response that you can make to the girl's expression.

Your response: _____

_____

_____

_____

_____

_____

DISCRIMINATING PERSONALIZING

Let us read again the learner's expression. Then let us read five alternative responses. We will ask you to rate these responses from 1.0 (very ineffective) to 5.0 (extremely effective) with 3.0 being minimally effective and 4.0 the response that communicates most effectively an understanding of where the learner is in relation to where she wants to be. Split the gaps between levels where appropriate.

"I don't like it here. Why can't I go to school in my own neighborhood?"

Your Rating

_____ 1. *"You feel bad about being here because you don't feel like it's your school and you want to feel like it is."*

_____ 2. *"You feel angry with things because you just haven't been able to get it 'together' here."*

_____ 3. *"You feel mad about this school because it doesn't feel like home here."*

_____ 4. *"You feel bad here because you haven't been able to feel at home."*

_____ 5. *"You feel angry about being here because it's not in your neighborhood."*

CHECKING OUT
PERSONALIZING DISCRIMINATIONS

The trained raters' ratings are listed in the table below. You may determine your discrimination score by obtaining the absolute deviations, adding them and dividing the total by 5. The result is your understanding discrimination score.

Teacher Responses	Ratings	Your Ratings	Difference (Deviations)
1	4.0	− _____	= _____
2	3.5	− _____	= _____
3	3.0	− _____	= _____
4	3.5	− _____	= _____
5	3.0	− _____	= _____

$$\text{Total} = \underline{\hspace{2cm}} = \frac{\underline{\hspace{2cm}}}{5}$$

Personalizing Discrimination Score

RECEIVING FEEDBACK

You will want further feedback to consolidate your learnings. Again, ratings above level 3.0 mean that the response is personalized while ratings below level 3.0 indicate that the response is not personalized. The highest level of personalizing understanding responds both to where the learner is and to where the learner wants to be. Rated at level 4.0, Response 1 is the model for personalizing understanding. All others fail to define the goals of helping from the learner's frame of reference. Accordingly, personalizing the feeling and meaning is rated at level 3.5 (Responses 2 and 4) while responding interchangeably to feeling and meaning is rated at level 3.0 (Responses 3 and 5).

UNDERSTANDING PERSONALIZING

You should have improved in your discrimination of personalizing understanding. The rating of 4.0 was assigned to the first response because it captured both where the learner is and where she wants to be. The third and fifth responses were rated at level 3.0 because they accurately reflected the feeling and meaning expressed by the learner. The second and fourth responses were rated at level 3.5 because they personalized the expression of the learner. If your discrimination score has not improved or if it deviates more than one-half level from these ratings, you should reread this chapter. If your discrimination score deviates less than one-half level, you are eligible to rate your level of understanding on the pre- and post-understanding tests. Again, you can develop your own scale for personalizing understanding. Your ratings of your personalizing responses should have improved significantly from before to after understanding training. You are now ready to personalize your understanding of your learners.

Level 3.0–Responding interchangeably to feeling and meaning
Level 3.5–Personalizing the feeling and meaning
Level 4.0–Personalizing understanding

Understanding Skills

Pre-Training   **Post-Training**

———Your Rating   ———Your Rating

MASTERING PERSONALIZING

Once you have mastered personalizing skills, you are one step closer toward your goal of effective teaching. Teachers who attend, respond and personalize are very effective (level 4.0). Personalizing skills prepare your learners for learning. The learners will trust you because you understand them and you can help them to understand themselves. Instead of dismissing your advice with a shrug of her shoulders, Janey, the class tomboy, will listen to you after you say, *"You feel afraid Janey, because the boys might not like you and you want them to."* Usually Peter looks at you with blank despair over his reading book. But he may feel a ray of hope when you say, *"You feel ashamed because you read so poorly out loud and you want to be able to read well in front of the class."*

Mastery of personalizing behaviors insures that you will deal effectively with classroom discipline problems. When you communicate your understanding of your learners, you help them to understand themselves. You will reduce the incidence of distracting student behaviors because you understand their learning problems too. You know where your learners are and you know where they want to go. How will you get them there?

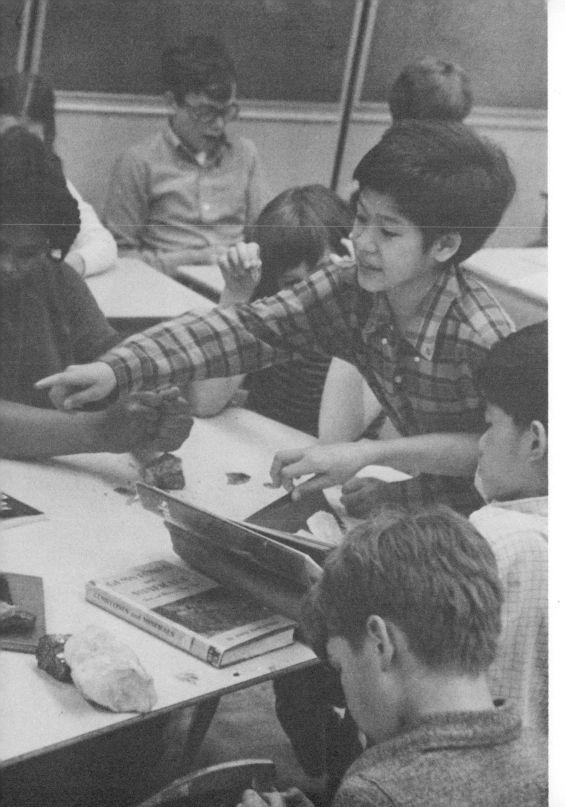

HELPING YOUR LEARNERS TO ACT UPON THEIR LEARNING —INITIATING SKILLS

EXPERIENCING INITIATING

"You know, a funny thing about this schooling bit. When kids are small—in elementary school—over 90 percent of the questions asked are asked by the kids. They are really curious about life. They really take the initiative to learn its mysteries. They almost don't need any initiative training. They just want to know how to get to be more effective.

Then, when they're college age, over 90 percent of the questions asked are asked by the teacher. And they're really not looking for answers. They're looking for the 'right answers' because they already know them. Something happens to the kids along the way. The natural, built-in inquisitiveness and initiative search for answers is extinguished—not by clean and sharp steps to truth but by stale, dull homilies which guide us not to life but to death.

Here, then, is our epitaph: 'From questions in search of answers to answers in search of questions.' To ask is to answer."

LEARNING INITIATING SKILLS

The highest level of initiative skills involves program development skills. Program development skills simply mean the skills involved in helping the learners get from where they are to where they want to be. Without program development skills, there is no culmination to the helping process. In addition, program development lays the basis for the teaching process. The teacher's initiating behavior facilitates the learners' ability to act. Before we begin the initiating module, let us check out the level of your initiating skills.

Teacher: **Helping Skills**   Attending   Responding   Personalizing   Initiating

Learners: **Learning Skills**   Exploring   Understanding   Acting

FORMULATING INITIATIVE RESPONSES

With good understanding responses, the learners can understand where they are in relation to where they want to be. But they may have difficulty in determining how to get there. It is the teacher's task to work with the learners to develop programs to get them from where they are to where they want to be. The source of the teacher's ability to develop programs is her understanding of where the learners are and where they want to be. We will now ask you to respond to a learner expression. In responding, please formulate in writing the response that communicates the greatest initiative in an understanding context. Assume that you have been interacting with the child for an hour or more. Write your response exactly as you would say it to the student. Do not simply describe what you would talk about. In the following exercise, a student comes to you and expresses the following concern.

"How can I get my English done when I don't even know how to study? Can you help me?"

Please formulate the most helpful initiative response that you can to the learner's expression.

*Your response:*_____

DISCRIMINATING INITIATING SKILLS

You may discover that it's not so easy to develop even the beginnings of a good initiative response. You may find yourself lapsing back into some of your old advice-type responses. You may have a *"feel"* for what you want to do to help the learner but somehow you cannot get it out in a way that he can use. If you cannot do so, all your learners may end up doing things that are not really going to help them get from where they are to where they want to be. We will read again the learner's expression. Then we will read five alternative teacher responses. We will ask you to rate these responses from 1.0 (very ineffective) to 5.0 (extremely effective) with 3.0 being minimally effective.

Now read once again the expression of the learner, after which we will read five alternative teacher responses. Please rate the responses from 1.0 to 5.0, with level 5.0 reflecting the response that most effectively communicates initiating. Split the gaps between levels where it is appropriate.

"How can I get my English done when I don't even know how to study? Can you help me?"

Your Rating

_____ 1. *"You should really try to study harder. The more you work, the better you will do."*

_____ 2. *"It's pretty upsetting to you because you don't know the first thing about studying and you really want to."*

_____ 3. *"The road of life is strewn with kids who never learned how to study."*

_____ 4. *"You feel pretty bad because studying has really got you down."*

_____ 5. *"You feel pretty frustrated because you can't study and you know you need to. There's a study program that some experts have worked out that's called the SQ3R method. First, you survey the material. Next, you ask questions about it. Then you read, recite and review. Now, let's take a look at this method and see if we can make it work for you."*

CHECKING OUT YOUR INITIATING DISCRIMINATIONS

Trained raters who have demonstrated the validity of their ratings in studies of helping and teaching outcome rated each of the teacher's attempts to communicate initiative. These ratings are listed in the table below. You may determine your discrimination score by obtaining your absolute deviations, adding them and dividing the total by 5. The result is your discrimination score.

Teacher Responses	Ratings	Your Ratings	Difference (Deviations)
1	2.0	− _____	= _____
2	4.0	− _____	= _____
3	1.0	− _____	= _____
4	3.0	− _____	= _____
5	5.0	− _____	= _____

Total = $\dfrac{\text{_____}}{5}$ = _____

Initiating Discrimination Score

LEARNING ABOUT INITIATING

An explanation of the ratings will help to prepare you for the training module. The rating of level 5.0 was assigned to Response 5 because it alone communicated initiative in an understanding context. It communicated an understanding of where the learner was and where he wanted to be. In addition, it communicated initiative by starting to lay out a program to get him from where he was to where he wanted to be. A rating of level 4.0 was assigned to Response 2 because it communicated a personalized understanding of where the learner was in relation to where he wanted to be. A rating of level 3.0 was assigned to Response 4 because it responded only to where the learner was. A rating of level 2.0 was assigned to Response 1 because, while it has some direction, the direction was not in an understanding context and therefore was not effective. Finally a rating of level 1.0 was assigned to Response 3 because it communicated neither responsiveness nor initiative to the learner. It had nothing to offer at all. While initiating will become clearer to you as you read this chapter, you should already have improved scores on the pre-test for initiating due to previous learnings. You now know something about initiating. You need to learn a lot more!

DEFINING THE GOAL

DEFINING GOALS
BY
ASKING BASIC QUESTIONS

There are several basic questions you must answer in order to define your learners' goals. These questions are reflected in the basic interrogatives: Who? What? When? Where? How? Why?

Who is involved? Is your learner going to move toward some private goal? Or are other people directly involved—parents, friends, children, even you yourself?

What is to be done? In other words, what learner behavior will characterize attainment of the goal? Running a mile in six minutes as a goal in physical fitness? Earning a high grade as a goal in an academic subject area?

When are actions to be performed? When will your learner take the first step toward the goal—right now, this afternoon, next week? And when will the goal be achieved —today, tomorrow, a month or even a year from now?

Where will the action take place? Will the learner's field of endeavor be at home? In school? In one particular room? In several locations?

How can the action be performed? Will the learner need any special expertise to move toward the goal? Will you need such expertise to help chart the new program of action? What methods and strategies are involved?

Why is the learner moving toward this goal? Are the benefits to be attained really measurable and meaningful? Does the learner fully understand how attainment of this goal will benefit her or him and pave the way for new goals and actions?

By asking and answering these basic questions, you can make sure that each learner's goal is defined in terms which are observable, measurable, useable and achievable. And such a definition, in turn, will insure that each learner's growth is as tangible and real as it is positive.

BEGINNING WITH
GOAL DEFINITION

Remember Paul, the learner you met in the last chapter who was troubled by his inability to make friends? As you saw, the highest level of personalized response to Paul's situation involved a statement along the lines of *"Paul, you feel vulnerable because you don't know how to make friends and you want very much to be able to."* Assuming that the teacher working with Paul had laid an adequate base for this response—through preliminary and continuous attending, observing and listening as well as through lower-level responses—Paul would recognize the way in which this personalized response captured and reflected his own experience of the world. He has come a long way. He is able to understand where he is in relation to where he wants to be. But he still needs help to get there. His goal, in general terms, is *"to be able to make friends."* But before he can act effectively, this goal must be defined in terms which are observable, measurable, functional and achievable.

DEFINING A LEARNER'S GOAL

The teacher working with Paul begins to help him define his goal by asking and answering the six basic questions we have outlined.

Who is involved? Paul is involved, of course, as are several of his peers in school —his potential friends. And the teacher is involved as a primary agent of change as well as someone who can provide continuing feedback and help.

What is to be done? Having friends might be defined as having people of the same age with whom you spend time and share leisure activities. Paul decides that he will consider his goal to have been reached when he can invite three different people his age over to his house—and have them come.

When are the actions to be performed? Paul will start at once and will give himself three weeks to reach his goal. To make the goal increasingly measurable, Paul and the teacher decide that each "invitation" must result in at least one hour of shared activity.

Where will the actions take place? Paul will be working on a planned sequence of activities both at school and at home. He will eventually invite the three other learners to visit him at home.

How can the actions be performed? In order to reach his goal of "friendship," Paul will need to develop his own array of interpersonal skills—the skills we all need to get along creatively and enjoyably with other people.

Why is the learner moving toward this goal? Paul's teacher makes sure that he sees quite clearly the tangible benefits he'll receive by reaching his goal; not only will he have at least three new friends, but he will also have the skills he can use at any future point to make other friends.

The answers to these six questions allow Paul and his teacher to arrive at a precise definition of Paul's goal—to be able to make new friends as measured by having three people his age visit him in his home for at least one hour during the next three weeks. As is clear, such a statement of goal is observable, measurable and functional. Once the program's action steps are in place, the goal will also be seen as quite achievable.

DEFINING THE GOAL FOR A GROUP

As with an individual, defining a goal for a group of learners begins with the answers to our six basic questions. Let's say that you have been working with a small group of younger learners who came to you originally because they were having trouble getting through their reading assignments. At first they tended to blame this situation on external causes: *"The stuff is so boring!"* and *"You just keep piling on the work!"* You attended, observed, listened, responded in terms of these learners' frames of reference and finally helped them to reach a more personalized understanding of where they are in terms of where they want to be. As one learner in the group put it, *"I feel dumb because I can't seem to get through the reading and I really want to be able to handle it all."* Now it's time to deal with the six questions.

Who is involved? Each learner in the group as well as you, the teacher whose assignments they find so troublesome.

What is to be done? The learners must be able to complete each reading assignment and answer some basic questions about what they've read.

When are actions to be performed? The learners will start this evening and will plan to reach their common goal within five days.

Where will the action take place? The learners will work both at school and at home.

How can the action be performed? The learners will undertake a systematic sequence of steps designed to bring them to their goal. These steps will involve taking time to work with the group during 10 successive class days.

Why are the learners moving toward this goal? The tangible benefits for the learners include better grades, more free time and greater self-confidence.

DEFINING YOUR OWN GOAL

Now it's time for you to practice your own skills by defining a goal for yourself. Let's assume that you set as a general goal *"to be able to put my new interpersonal skills to use."* Given this general indication of where you want to be in the future, how would you answer our six questions in order to define your own goal?

Who is involved?_____

_____

What is to be done?_____

_____

When are actions to be performed?_____

_____

Where will the action take place?_____

_____

How can the action be performed?_____

_____

Why are you moving toward this goal?_____

_____

Remember—your aim here is to arrive at a definition of your own goal which is stated in terms that are measurable, observable, functional and achievable.

DEFINING A GOAL IS JUST A START

By way of feedback, here are some sample responses you might have made to the six questions concerning your own goal. These are not, of course, the only possible answers; but they do serve to reflect the qualities which any definition of goals must possess.

Who is involved? You are, of course, and so are those learners who will be the recipients or beneficiaries of your interpersonal skills.

What is to be done? Since your aim is to put your interpersonal skills to use, you might decide that you want to be able to respond accurately to each of your learners.

When are actions to be performed? You will start at once and will endeavor to respond to all of your learners individually within the next month.

Where will the action take place? You will be using your skills in your own classroom.

How can the action be performed? To reach your goal, you will have to chart a careful sequence of steps for yourself. And this means that you will first have to complete your acquisition of the initiative or program development skills outlined in this chapter.

Why are you moving toward this goal? You may well have a number of personal and specific reasons for wishing to reach this goal. In general, the effective use of interpersonal skills will enable you to teach more effectively by making sure that you are reaching and helping each learner in ways that both he or she and you can recognize. Such skills insure a minimum of wasted time and energy and a maximum of creative growth.

Now you understand how a goal must be defined. But goal definition is just a start. There is a good deal more about initiating that you still must learn.

ESTABLISHING THE FIRST STEP

THE REQUIREMENTS
OF A FIRST STEP

Defining goals for learners is essential. But it is not, of course, sufficient. The next thing you must do is help each learner to chart an appropriate **first step** leading toward the goal. This first step should be so simple that the learner can take it easily; thus she or he will gain valuable self confidence (as well as confidence in you as *"navigator")* and will be encouraged to take additional steps. This first step—like all succeeding ones—should move the learner in a direct line toward the goal. It should, like the goal itself, be reducible to terms which are measurable, observable and functional as well as achievable. And it should take fully into account just where the learner presently is in terms of relevant skills and overall frame of reference; a good first step for a learner who wished to master a foreign language, then, would **not** be to take an expensive, privately-sponsored course in advanced French given in a city some 30 miles away.

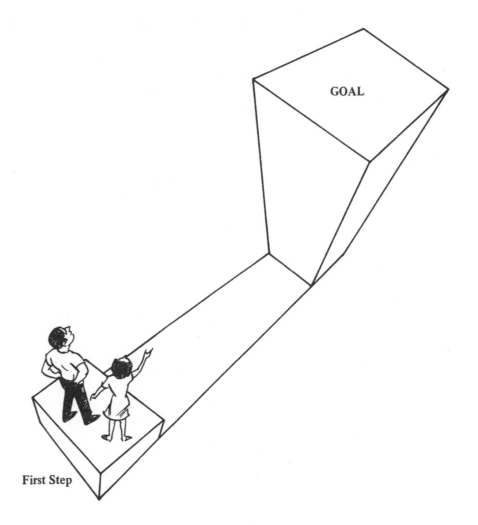

GOAL

First Step

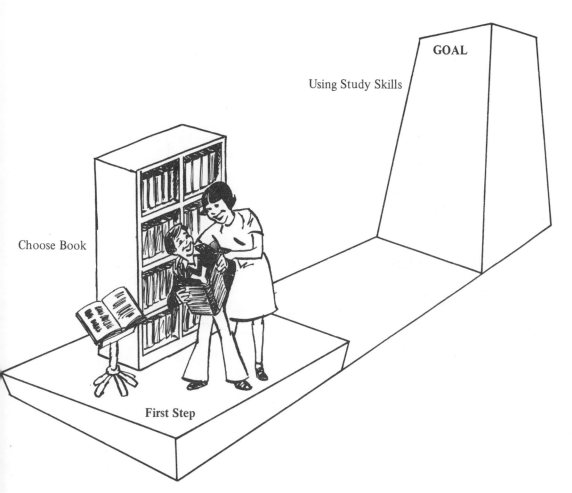

GOAL

Using Study Skills

Choose Book

First Step

DEVELOPING THE FIRST STEP
FOR LEARNERS

The teacher working with Paul understood the critical nature of the first step in terms of Paul's success in making friends. The teacher also saw that Paul did not even have the basic skills needed to meet people, much less develop a true friendship with them. Working together, this teacher and Paul decided that a good first step would involve Paul's acquisition of simple *"greeting"* skills— saying *"hello"* and giving his name, for example. Such a step would be easy for Paul to complete and would move him directly toward his goal. To insure that the step was measurable, they decided that Paul would demonstrate his new skills by greeting at least one new person in each of his classes each day for three days in a row.

Working with your hypothetical group of learners who lack study skills, you might decide that their best first step involves each of them choosing one short book (no more than 60 pages) that they want or need to read. Here again, you focus on a task which is directly relevant to the group's common goal and which involves observable and measurable behavior. In addition, it is a step which each member of the group can take easily.

DEVELOPING YOUR OWN FIRST STEP

Now, what about your own goal of putting to use your new interpersonal skills. You have already defined this goal in appropriate terms.

There are, of course, several ways in which you might have outlined your first step. One such way might have involved a statement along the lines of *"My first step will be to respond to one learner in one class tomorrow."* This would move you directly toward your goal of responding to all of your learners in the next month. It is also a step which you can take easily and which is both measurable and observable.

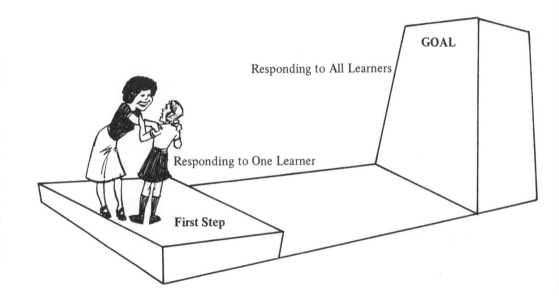

GOAL

Responding to All Learners

Responding to One Learner

First Step

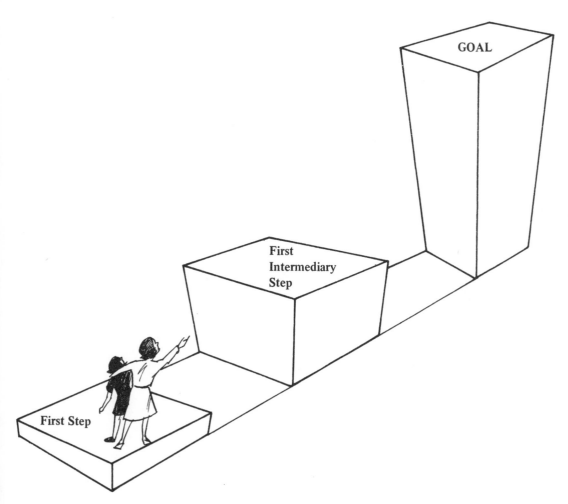

First Step

First
Intermediary
Step

GOAL

ESTABLISHING THE
FIRST INTERMEDIARY STEP

REQUIREMENTS OF THE
FIRST INTERMEDIARY STEP

Few meaningful goals can be achieved in a single step. In fact, trying to achieve a goal in one huge step is the single most common cause of failure to achieve a goal at all! In most if not every case, you will want to help your learners chart intermediary steps to bridge the gulf between where their first step leaves them and where they ultimately want to be. Initially, then, you will want to establish a **first intermediary step**. This step should be partway between the first step and the goal. While it is not essential that this step be precisely half-way between the first step and the goal (since you will be establishing other intermediary steps), you will understand the process of program development better (and learn to sharpen your own step-setting aim) if you do aim at an approximate half-way point.

Like the goal itself and the first step, this first intermediary step should be articulated in terms which are observable, measurable, functional and achievable. Only in this way can the learner know when he or she has taken the step and where she or he now is in relation to the goal.

166

DEVELOPING
THE FIRST INTERMEDIARY STEP
FOR LEARNERS

The teacher working with Paul decided that a good first intermediary step would involve Paul's acquisition of basic *"talking"* skills which would allow him to express himself to other people. Seeking again to make sure that the step was measurable, Paul and the teacher decided that his *"talking"* skills would be adequate when he could engage five other people his own age in conversations of at least five minutes each. They planned to have Paul complete this step by the end of the first 10 days.

Working with your group of learners on their reading task, you might outline a first intermediary step which involved each of them reading the book. Like Paul's first intermediary step, this is a step your learners can take successfully once they have completed some additional intermediary steps.

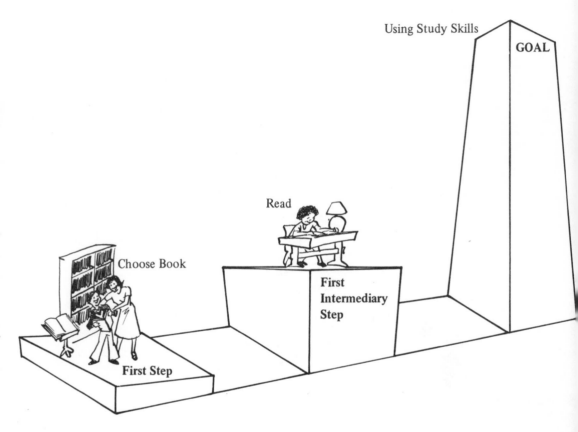

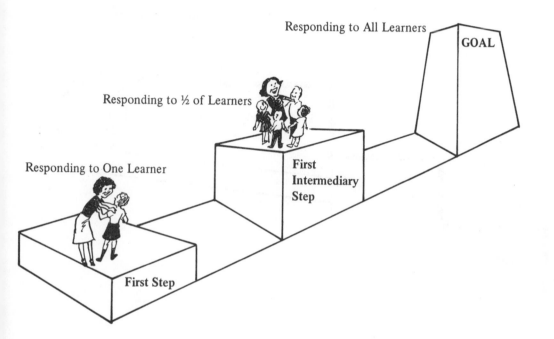

Responding to All Learners

GOAL

Responding to ½ of Learners

Responding to One Learner

First Intermediary Step

First Step

DEVELOPING YOUR OWN FIRST INTERMEDIARY STEP

Now, what about your own program designed to help you reach your goal of responding to every learner in the next month? You have already outlined your first step. Now do the same for your first intermediary step.

Again, there are several ways in which you might chart this step. One such way would involve a statement along the lines of *"My first intermediary step will be to respond individually to one-half of my learners within the next two weeks."* Such a step would move you directly toward your goal and would involve behaviors which are eminently observable and measurable.

ESTABLISHING ADDITIONAL INTERMEDIARY STEPS

ADDITIONAL INTERMEDIARY STEPS

Once you have established the first step and the first intermediary step leading toward a learner's goal, you need to bridge the inevitable *"gaps"* with sufficient **additional intermediary steps** to assure that the learner moves surely and successfully in the direction of the goal. As with the goal itself, the first step and the first intermediary step, these new intermediary steps must involve specific, measurable and observable behaviors for the learner.

There is no hard-and-fast number of intermediary steps that an effective program must have. Rather, your concern should be to avoid any gaps which are wide enough for the learner to *"fall through."*

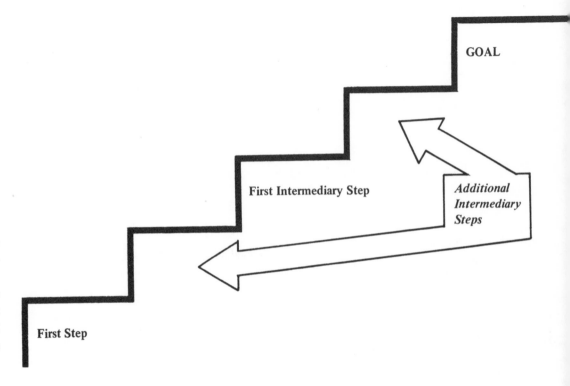

GOAL

First Intermediary Step

Additional Intermediary Steps

First Step

DEVELOPING
ADDITIONAL INTERMEDIARY STEPS
FOR LEARNERS

Paul's teacher had already outlined Paul's first step—to acquire *"greeting"* skills—and his first intermediary step—to acquire *"talking"* skills. But a shy learner like Paul cannot be expected to *"leap"* from the point where he can greet someone to the point where he can carry on a conversation with that person. The teacher realizes this and establishes two additional intermediary steps. After Paul acquires greeting skills, he will work to develop attending skills which allow him to become aware of other people's frames of reference; and after he acquires talking skills, he will develop responding skills which allow him to respond in terms of the other people's frames of reference.

Working with your group of learners on their reading problem, you might decide that additional intermediary steps would involve your delivery to them of specific study skills: techniques of surveying material, of reading to find answers, of reciting important information and of reviewing material. Your first step was to have them choose a book. A new intermediary step could be to have them survey their books. Then comes your first intermediary step: having the group ask questions. Following this, other new intermediary steps might involve having members read the book to get answers to their questions, recite important facts and review what they have read. They could then transfer their skills to their regular assignments with a high probability of reaching their original goal.

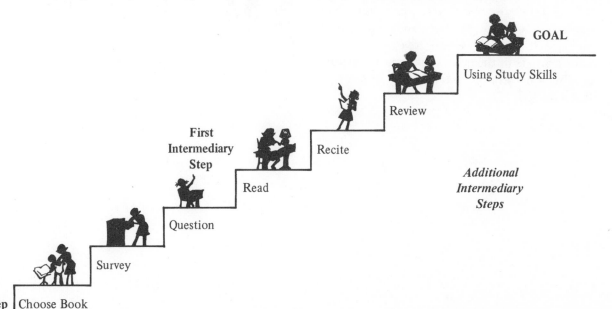

DEVELOPING YOUR OWN
ADDITIONAL INTERMEDIARY STEPS

Returning to your own program designed to help you put your interpersonal skills to use, what additional intermediary steps might you develop?

Your intermediary steps should be designed to bridge any gaps in your existing program. Your goal, you remember, is to use your interpersonal skills by responding to each of your learners once during the next month. As indicated, your first step might be to respond to one learner in one class; and your first intermediary step might be to respond to one-half of your learners during the next two weeks. Given these steps, you could chart at least two additional intermediary steps: to respond to one-quarter of your learners in the next week; and to respond to three-quarters of your learners in the next three weeks.

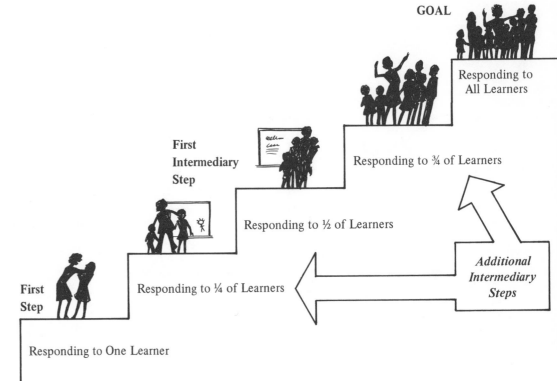

GOAL

Responding to All Learners

First Intermediary Step

Responding to ¾ of Learners

Responding to ½ of Learners

Additional Intermediary Steps

First Step

Responding to ¼ of Learners

Responding to One Learner

ESTABLISHING SUBSTEPS

THE REQUIREMENTS
FOR SUBSTEPS

At this point in developing a learner's program, you have anywhere from three to a dozen or more major steps: the first one, the first intermediary one and additional intermediary ones. What you need to do now is look at each of these major steps as a mini-goal in its own right. Paul needs to develop greeting skills. That step becomes a mini-goal. To reach it, he must recognize and be able to take the specific **substeps** leading up to it. These substeps comprise the specific and detailed behaviors which characterize achievement of the mini-goal—they're what must be done to *"take"* the step!

Great, huh? Just when you thought you had gotten down to the fine print, we introduce a whole new level of detail. But these are the details which make the real difference between a program that looks good but leads nowhere and a program that actually works! This is the *"nitty gritty"* level of program development so often ignored by people long on good intentions and short on commitment —and yet the level that ultimately makes the difference between learner failure and learner success!

To develop the substeps which will allow a learner to take major steps successfully (in other words, to reach the mini-goals), you need to look at each of these major steps and ask *"What must the learner do specifically in order to complete this step?"* The details of your answer are the details you need to design the appropriate substeps.

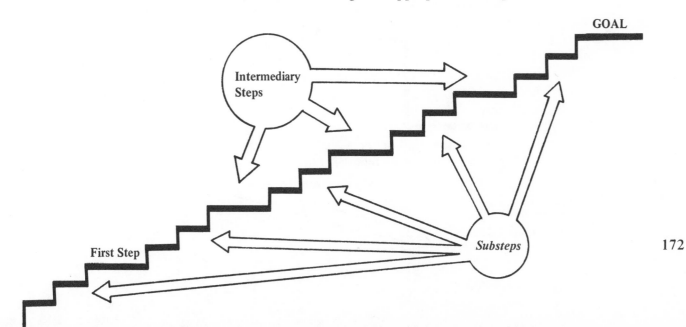

172

DEVELOPING SUBSTEPS FOR THE GROUP

Working with your hypothetical group of learners who have been experiencing difficulty in reading, you have established a sequence of five major steps: choosing a short book; surveying the book; developing questions to be answered; reading the material; reciting the answers to the questions; and reviewing the material. Now you might chart the specific substeps this program would require. Your program might then look like the one below.

Step 7:
Goal: Using study skills

Review
Recite
Read
Question
Survey

Step 6:   Review

Return to book to strengthen knowledge
Determine "weak" areas

Step 5:   Recite

Ask and answer questions verbally
Put aside book and papers, ask "What do I know?"

Step 4:   Read

Write down answers when found
Keep questions handy

Step 3:   Question

Write down questions
Ask "What do I need to know?"

Step 2:   Survey

Read first and last paragraphs in every chapter
Read title, covers, table of contents

Step 1:   Choose book

Determine interest
Determine availability

Substeps

173

DEVELOPING YOUR OWN SUBSTEPS

Now, what about your own program for using your interpersonal skills with your learners? Use a separate sheet of paper to draw an outline of both your major steps and the appropriate substeps you feel should be included. When you have finished, check the outline below to see the way in which one sample program might include appropriate substeps.

Step 5:
Goal: Responding to all learners

Formulating individual responses
Identifying frames of reference
Attending, observing, listening

Step 4:   Responding to ¾ of learners

Formulating individual responses
Identifying frames of reference
Attending, observing, listening

Step 3:   Responding to ½ of learners

Formulating individual responses
Identifying frames of reference
Identifying frames of reference
Attending, observing, listening

Substeps

Step 2:   Responding to ¼ of learners

Formulating individual responses
Identifying frames of reference
Attending, observing, listening

Step 1:   Responding to one learner

Formulate response
Identify frame of reference
Attend, observe, listen
Select learner

174

DEVELOPING PAUL'S SUBSTEPS

The outline below shows how Paul's teacher might chart the substeps and major steps which make up Paul's program. The steps assigned numbers include the first step, the first intermediary step and all additional intermediary steps. Below each are listed some specific substeps.

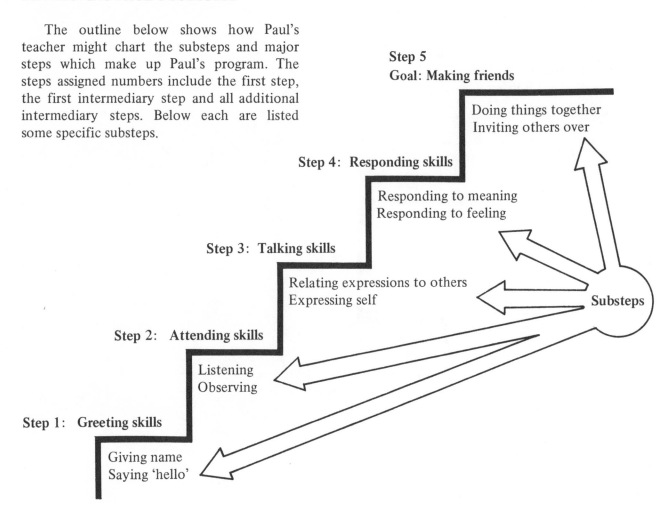

Step 5
Goal: Making friends

Doing things together
Inviting others over

Step 4: Responding skills

Responding to meaning
Responding to feeling

Step 3: Talking skills

Relating expressions to others
Expressing self

Substeps

Step 2: Attending skills

Listening
Observing

Step 1: Greeting skills

Giving name
Saying 'hello'

PUTTING YOUR SKILLS TOGETHER

OVERVIEW OF
PROGRAM DEVELOPMENT PHASES

Program development skills, as you have seen, bridge the gap between where the learners are and where they want to be. The response *"You feel_____ because you (cannot)_____and you want to_____"* gives the general direction for the program. Beginning with this general direction, you now have the skills you need to develop step-by-step programs of action.

First, determine the learner's general goal from the phrase *"... you want to_____ _____."*

Second, define this goal in terms which are measurable, observable, functional and achievable by asking and answering the questions involving the six basic interrogatives:

Who? What? When? Where? How? Why?

Third, establish the first step, making sure that it takes into account where the learner presently is in terms of a particular deficit or inability (from the phrase *"... you cannot _____."*) This and all subsequent steps must, like the goal, be observable, measurable, functional and achievable.

Fourth, establish the first intermediary step partway to the learner's goal.

Fifth, establish additional intermediary steps which serve to bridge significant gaps in the program.

Sixth, treat each of the major steps you have developed as a *"mini-goal"* and develop the specific substeps the learner will need to take.

PUTTING ALL YOUR
PROGRAM DEVELOPMENT
SKILLS TOGETHER

Obviously, you can develop the programs for Paul, the reading group or yourself in still more detail. The more detail that you develop, the higher the probability of your success in achieving the program's goals. Some goals may require a special expertise. In that case, develop a program for yourself or the learners to find out the information necessary to develop a program in an area requiring special expertise. However, you may be surprised at how much of your program involves common sense: you must walk before you run and stand before you walk. Try developing a detailed program for Mary, the girl we met in Chapter 5, from the additive response developed earlier by the effective teacher.

"You feel lost right now because you haven't been able to handle your school assignments and you want very much to be able to handle them all the time."

Go back and review the early exchanges with Mary if you wish to refresh your memory. Use all of the steps that were used in developing a program for Paul. This program does involve a goal that you should know something about—school.

CHECKING OUT
PUTTING YOUR PROGRAM
DEVELOPMENT SKILLS TOGETHER

Here is a program that an effective teacher might have developed for Mary following the principles of program development. You see that this is a common sense problem. It does not, for example, require any special knowledge of study skills, although every effective teacher should have an effective program for study skills. Again, the program can be developed in greater detail. Indeed, if you wish to conquer program development skills, make each one of these steps a subgoal and develop at least a simple three-step program to achieve the subgoal.

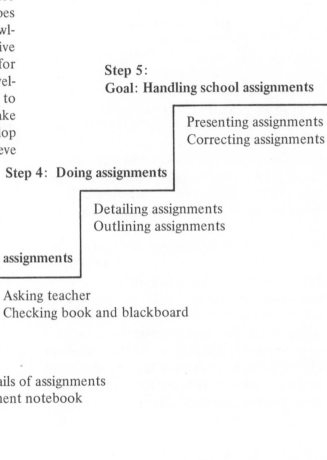

Step 5:
Goal: Handling school assignments

Presenting assignments
Correcting assignments

Step 4: Doing assignments

Detailing assignments
Outlining assignments

Step 3: Checking out assignments

Asking teacher
Checking book and blackboard

Step 2: Writing down assignments

Recording details of assignments
Having assignment notebook

Step 1: Listening for assignments

Observing
Attending

PRACTICING YOUR
PROGRAM DEVELOPMENT SKILLS
WITH YOUR LEARNERS

Now let us transfer your program development skills into the classroom again. Continue working with the learners with whom you have been successful in responding. Identify an individual learner with a particular concern or problem. Use the additive responses which you are able to develop from your responsive base to define the goal and the first step of the program for this learner. Now develop an intermediary step partway between the first step and the goal. Then, continue to develop intermediary steps until you have exhausted all major steps in the program. Now, make each of these steps a subgoal for another program. Check to see if you have left any important steps out. If the space between steps is too great, the learner will not be able to achieve his or her goal. Always remember to make each of the steps observable and measurable, functional and achievable. When you can develop programs for your learners with some facility, then you are ready for the fine details of curriculum development.

PRACTICING DEVELOPING STEPS
IN THE CLASSROOM

Now practice developing steps for a large group of learners in the classroom. You might involve the learners in developing steps to achieve group goals. Class task forces can be established for the development of different steps. Or the class members might even vote upon what steps are to be included. The steps will enable your learners to achieve their goals.

PRACTICING INITIATING FULLY IN THE CLASSROOM

Now put your goal-setting and program-development skills together by initiating fully in the classroom. This means utilizing all of your goal-setting and program-development skills to achieve the goals that you have personalized for your learners. In addition, it means developing time lines, attending to the steps taken, differentially reinforcing movement toward or away from the goal and correcting the steps. This will enable you to recycle the learning process, with the feedback from learner action stimulating new exploration, more accurate understanding and more effective action.

PRACTICING MAKING APPLICATIONS IN THE CLASSROOM

Again, see if you can make several more applications of initiating in the classroom. Include the interactions between learners as well as between you and the learners. Try to make sure that you have initiated effectively with each learner and each group of learners, helping them to achieve their personalized goals for each new unit of learning. That way you will insure that the learners achieve learning goals that they have set for themselves. Later on, you may want to teach your learners directly how to initiate steps to achieve their own goals in learning.

POST-TRAINING
INITIATING ASSESSMENT

USING YOUR INITIATING SKILLS

Now let us make a post-training assessment of your initiating skills. We will ask you once again to initiate with the learner as fully as you can. Remember to initiate in an understanding context. Assume that you have been interacting with one girl for an hour or more. Write your response exactly as you would say it to the student. Do not describe what you would talk about. In the following exercise, a learner expresses the following experience.

"I've worked very hard to learn how to add and subtract and to multiply and divide. But I get messed up when you give me problems where I have to do all these things."

Please formulate the most helpful response that you can to the girl's expression.

*Your response:*_____

_____

_____

_____

_____

DISCRIMINATING INITIATING SKILLS

Let us read again the learner's expression. Then let us read five alternative responses. We will ask you to rate the responses from 1.0 (very ineffective) to 5.0 (extremely effective), with 5.0 reflecting the response that most effectively communicates initiating. Split the gaps between levels where it is appropriate.

"I've worked very hard to learn how to add and subtract and to multiply and divide. But I get messed up when you give me problems where I have to do all of these things."

Your Rating

_____1. *"You're lost because you don't know the order of the operations and you want to learn them."*

_____2. *"You feel confused because you don't know the order of operations and you want to. Now, there's an old expression that will help you: 'My Dear Aunt Sally' means that you do the operations in the following order: multiply, divide, add, subtract."*

_____3. *"Girls usually have trouble with math and you shouldn't worry about it."*

_____4. *"That's something that you just have to keep working very hard at until you get a 'feel' for it."*

_____5. *"You feel confused because of all the operations."*

CHECKING OUT YOUR INITIATIVE DISCRIMINATIONS

The trained raters' ratings are listed in the table below. You may determine your discrimination score by obtaining the absolute deviations, adding them and dividing the total by 5. The result is your initiating discrimination score.

Teacher Responses	Ratings	Your Ratings	Difference (Deviations)
1	4.0	− _____	= _____
2	5.0	− _____	= _____
3	1.0	− _____	= _____
4	2.0	− _____	= _____
5	3.0	− _____	= _____

Total = _____ = _____
                5   *Initiating Discrimination Score*

RECEIVING FEEDBACK

Additional feedback on your ratings may help to reinforce your learnings about initiating. Again, ratings at level 5.0 mean that the teacher has helped the learner to develop a step-by-step program for how to get from where she is to where she wants to be (Response 2). This is the highest level of initiating. Everything else fails to get the learner to her goal. Accordingly, Response 1 personalizes the learner's understanding and is rated at level 4.0. Response 5 is interchangeable with the feeling and meaning expressed by the learner and is rated at level 3.0. Response 4 is a guidance response and is rated at level 2.0 and Response 3 is irrelevant and is rated at level 1.0.

UNDERSTANDING INITIATING

You should have improved in your discrimination of initiating. The rating of 5.0 was assigned to the second response because it incorporated how to get from where the learner was to where she wanted to be. The first response was assigned a rating of 4.0 because it included an understanding of where the learner was in relation to where the learner wanted to be. The fifth response was rated at level 3.0 because it responded to where the learner was. The fourth response was rated at level 2.0 because, while it had some direction, the direction was not in an understanding context and therefore was not effective. Finally, a rating of level 1.0 was assigned to the third response because it communicated neither responsiveness nor initiative; in fact, it did little more than reflect the speaker's latent sexism! If your discrimination score has not improved or if it deviates more than one-half level from the ratings, then you should reread this chapter. If your discrimination score deviates less than one-half level, then you are eligible to rate your level of initiating on the pre- and post-initiating tests. Again, you could develop your own scale for initiating. Your rating of your initiating responses should have improved significantly from before to after initiating training. You are now ready to initiate with your students.

Level 4.0—Making additive understanding responses that develop the goal
Level 4.5—Defining the goal in operational terms
Level 5.0—Developing a step-by-step program to achieve the goal

Initiating Skills

Pre-Training   **Post-Training**

_____Your Rating   _____Your Rating

MASTERING INITIATING

Once you have mastered initiating, you have taken the final step toward effective interpersonal classroom skills. Teachers who attend, respond, personalize and initiate are extremely effective (level 5.0) in preparing their learners to learn.

With your initiating skills you become the source of direction to your learners. They know that you care about them. They know that you understand how they feel. They know that you are ready to teach them. So when Angelo swears, you help him to understand what he needs to learn when you say, *"You feel angry because you did it wrong and you want to be able to do it right. Swearing won't help you, instead try hooking up the two red wires."* And when Karen has trouble with her division, you will use your initiating skills to break the task down into small, sequential steps. Then she can learn to divide correctly.

Remember that your effectiveness in initiating is totally dependent upon your effectiveness in attending, responding and personalizing. You never get so good at initiating that you do not have to check back with the learners' experiences. Indeed, there is no effective initiative in the absence of effective responsiveness.

PREPARING YOUR LEARNERS FOR LEARNING

REALIZING THAT TEACHING IS FOR THE LEARNERS

In teaching, it is important to get the learners ready for learning. You do this by entering your learners' frames of reference. You find out where your learners are when you correct their unit tests. You find out how your learners feel when you pass back the unit test. Some of your learners may even approach you after class about their test results: *"I did O.K., huh?"* or *"Boy, I really blew that one!"* You know where your learners are in relation to what you have just taught. You know how they feel about what they have learned. It is important to use your interpersonal skills to concentrate upon where the learners are. So often, we find that the teaching process operates independent of the learners. So often, too, we find that the teacher puts the emphasis upon the process of teaching and not the learning outcome; they put the program rather than themselves *"out front."* In this manner, the program is the only thing *"on the line."* You will want to put yourself *"on the line"* because you have learned interpersonal skills that help you teach the learners.

ATTENDING AND RESPONDING
SO THAT YOUR LEARNERS EXPLORE

Use the interpersonal skills which you
have learned to emphasize the learners' growth
and development. Attend to them—observe
them—listen to them. You might hear them
say:

"Why is this wrong? It looks right to me!
"Nuts! Who needs it?"
"Not again! And I studied!"

Here you see that most of your learners
are really down. All you have to do is watch
their faces and listen to their comments. This
feedback becomes your richest source of
learning about your learners. All teaching
begins with attending to the learners. Attending is the basis for responding accurately to
their experiences. Teachers who have not
learned interpersonal skills may ignore their
learners' feelings about not doing well on the
unit test. Or they may say, *"Next time you'll*
have to study harder." This high initiative-low
responsive statement does not provide the
learners with the direction they need because
it does not come from their frame of reference. They think they did study. The teacher
who uses interpersonal skills correctly can
respond, *"You feel badly because you didn't*
do well on the test." Then the learners are
ready to explore why they didn't do well on
the test.

PERSONALIZING SO YOUR LEARNERS UNDERSTAND

Your responding skills have allowed your learners to explore their problem of failing the unit test.

"I thought I knew how to do it."

"I studied for over an hour."

"I didn't know what to do first."

Responding accurately provides us with the material which we need to help the learners to understand themselves. Using your interpersonal skills you may begin to personalize your learners' experience by saying, *"You feel confused because you thought you knew what to do but you really didn't."*

The learners can understand themselves in terms of where they are in relation to where they want to be.

"I got all the measurements wrong."

"That metric system!"

"It's hard to learn!"

When you personalize the problem, your learners can understand the goals that you set when you say: *"You feel badly because you cannot convert to metric measure and you want to be able to."*

They are now oriented to a goal. They have direction. It remains only for you to provide them with a road map of the steps to doing better on the retest.

INITIATING SO YOUR LEARNERS ACT

Now you use your initiative skills to provide the steps your learners need to learn the pieces they are missing. Spending several days teaching metric measure provides the systematic program to meet the learners' need. They have failed a test because they had not learned metric measure. That is where they are. Your program will take them step-by-step to where they want to go: they want to be able to use metric measure. In this way, we build success into our learners' lives. We are teaching them what they need to know.

Then you can say to your learners:

"You feel really good because you did so well on the unit retest."

UNDERSTANDING LEARNER DIFFERENCES

When you use your interpersonal skills with learners, you realize the enormous differences within as well as between learners. You see clearly that different learners are functioning at different levels. Indeed, you see clearly that at different times the same learners are functioning at different levels. Nevertheless, it is important to understand that over time the learners' levels of physical, emotional, social and intellectual functioning will converge. In other words, significant growth in any one of these dimensions—physical, emotional, social or intellectual—will give impetus to growth in the other dimensions. Similarly, significant deterioration or retardation in any of these dimensions will tend to contribute to the deterioration or retardation of development in the other dimensions. Accordingly, we must do everything in our power to facilitate the learners' growth. We must use our interpersonal skills.

RELATING INTERPERSONAL SKILLS TO INDIVIDUAL NEEDS

It is absolutely critical that you use your interpersonal skills to individualize your treatment of different learners or the same learners at different times. It may be helpful to think of this differential treatment in terms of the phases of learning. Some learners may be functioning at low levels with regard to a particular area of learning. It is important to emphasize the exploration phase with low-level functioning learners. In an atmosphere of attending and responding, the learners have an extensive opportunity to explore, experience and experiment with the learning material or other concerns at hand. With higher-level functioning learners, you may move more quickly through the exploration phase. You may, instead, stress the responding and understanding skills that enable the learners to develop an understanding of where they are in relation to where they want to be. However, if you cannot easily arrive at such an understanding, it may be necessary to recycle a more fully developed exploration process. The goal for the highest-level functioning learners is to develop an achievable goal and an action program to get there. Accordingly, you may move swiftly through the exploration and understanding phases with these action-oriented, high-level functioning learners.

USING YOUR INTERPERSONAL SKILLS IN THE CLASSROOM

Remember, all of the principles of individualizing learning experiences hold for groups of learners as well as individual learners. You apply exactly the same skills to groups as you do to individuals. You treat a group as you do individuals, for a group is no more than multiple individuals. Thus you can attend, respond, personalize and initiate with individuals within groups and with groups of individuals. Later on, you will learn how to organize your classes into groups of individuals, depending upon your learning tasks. You use your interpersonal skills fully to enter the learner's frame of reference so that you can employ your teaching skills to develop and deliver your content to meet that learner's frame of reference.

HELPING YOURSELF

In order to use all of your interpersonal skills effectively, you must first have yourself *"together."* You must be *"together"* physically. It takes an enormous energy level to discharge the responsibilities of a teacher. At a minimum, you should develop some physical programs—like running—that develop your cardiovascular functioning. The coordination between your heart and your lungs is the best index of your overall physical health. With physical health, anything is possible! Without physical health, nothing is possible!

It takes accurate interpersonal and emotional skills to be an effective teacher. Learning these skills has been the message of this book. To be understanding of and helpful to people you are paid to serve is only to live as a decent and responsible human being. Sounds simple—yet it takes practice to become a decent and responsible human being.

It takes acute intellectual skills to be an effective teacher. It is not enough to know the facts of life—or even the concepts of life; you must know its principles and, most important, be able to operationalize its skills objectives and develop systematic programs to achieve these skills objectives. These are additional learning tasks of **The Skills of Teaching: Interpersonal Skills.**

Before you can help someone, you must first help yourself.

DISCOVERING THE PRINCIPLES OF TEACHING

When you think back to all of the educational activities in which you engage, you can now give them a new meaning. Whether you are developing an educational curriculum, diagnosing your learners' level of educational achievement, setting performance objectives or methodologies or organizing and managing your classroom activities, you can assess them in terms of their essential teaching dimensions: (1) do these activities respond to where the learners are? (2) do they express an understanding of where the learners want to be in relation to where they are? (3) do they initiate programs for how to get the learners from where they are to where they want to be? If your educational activities incorporate these essential dimensions, then you will achieve your educational objectives. If your educational activities are deficient in one or more of these dimensions, then you will not achieve your educational objectives.

USING YOUR SCALE FOR
DISCRIMINATING EFFECTIVENESS

Early in the book, during your preliminary discrimination training, you learned to discriminate communications roughly. Throughout the book, you have developed your own scale for making ratings. This scale may have been helpful to you in making ratings in your learning programs. Let us review the full scale.

Level 1.0—No expression or expression unrelated to learners
Level 1.5—Expression related to learners—usually poor guidance
Level 2.0—Responding to content—usually some guidance for learners
Level 2.5—Responding to feeling of learners
Level 3.0—Responding interchangeably to feeling and meaning of learners
Level 3.5—Personalizing the meaning of learners
Level 4.0—Personalizing understanding of learners' goal
Level 4.5—Defining the goal in terms of steps to learners' goal
Level 5.0—Developing a step-by-step program to achieve learners' goal

UNDERSTANDING THE LEVELS
OF COMMUNICATION

Since you have learned to communicate at high levels, making fine discriminations has become relatively easy. It may be worth elaborating upon the levels of communicating in some detail.

Level 1.0. These responses are low on responsiveness and low on initiative. They completely miss the feeling and meaning expressed by the learners. They do not give any direction to the learners. Such responses often take the form of meaningless questions or homilies. They are not effective at all because they neither understand where the learners are or where they want to be.

Level 2.0. These responses are low on responsiveness and high on initiative. They miss all or most of the feeling and meaning expressed by the learners. They do, however, give some form of guidance or direction. Such responses often take the form of advice or teacher encouragement. They are ineffective because, while they communicate some attempt to develop a direction toward where the learners want to be, they do not communicate an understanding of where learners are.

Level 3.0. These responses are high on responsiveness and low on initiative. They accurately capture the feeling and meaning expressed by the learners. They do not, however, give any direction. Such responses can fit the format, *"You feel_____ because _____ ."* This is a minimally effective response because it communicates at least an understanding of where the learners are.

Level 4.0. These responses are high on responsiveness and high on initiative. They personalize the understanding of the feeling and meaning beyond the level expressed by the learners. They also supply direction and guidance. Such responses can fit the format, *"You feel_____ because you (cannot) _____ and you want to_____ ."* These responses are very effective because they understand where the learners are and where they want to go.

Level 5.0. These responses are very high on responsiveness and very high on initiative. They accurately express the feeling and meaning of the learners' experience at a much deeper level than the learners expressed it. The direction they give clearly shows an understanding of the gap between where the learners are and where they want to be in their total life situation. In addition, they provide a means to get there. The responses fitting the format *"You feel_____ because you (cannot)_____ and you want to_____ ,"* are complemented by the systematic efforts to develop a program to achieve the learners' goal. This is an extremely effective response because it not only identifies where the learners are and where they want to be but points toward a means to get the learners to where they want to be.

UNDERSTANDING THE INTERCHANGEABLE RESPONSE

In making your ratings, do the following: look to see if the response accurately captures the feeling and meaning expressed by the learners. One of the most effective ways of doing this is to make a determination of whether the response could fit into the level 3.0 format, *"You feel_____ because _____."* Again, an interchangeable response means that the teacher has at least heard what the learners have expressed. Whatever else the teacher goes on to do will be dependent upon the accuracy with which she has heard and communicated her understanding. Anything is possible with an interchangeable response. It is not insured or even probable. But it is possible. **Nothing is possible without an interchangeable response!**

If the response does not fit the interchangeable format, give it a 1.0 or a 2.0, depending upon whether or not the response supplies advice or guidance. If it does fit the format, give it a 3.0 or 4.0, depending upon whether or not the response supplies advice or guidance. If it gives both understanding and direction at very deep and broad levels and provides the means to accomplish the learners' goals, give it a 5.0. Again, you may split the gap between the levels 1.0 and 5.0. That is, you may assign ratings at levels 1.5, 2.5, 3.5, or 4.5 if you feel this is necessary.

TESTING THE ACCURACY OF YOUR UNDERSTANDING

Now we are going to get another index of your interpersonal skills. First, after you formulate your communication responses to learner expressions, you will assign a rating to the teacher responses in the discrimination index in the first part of the section. Next, you will determine your discrimination score by comparing your ratings to our ratings and using the procedures described. You should find that your discrimination score is half a level or lower, that is .5 or lower. If your discrimination score is a half-level or lower, then you will be eligible to rate your own communications. If your discrimination score is .6 or higher, you should reread the preliminary training in rating in the early pages of the section. If you miss two or more of the same type of responses, by a level or more each, then reread the appropriate part of the explanation section in the pre-training and the appropriate parts of the responsiveness and initiative communication training.

**POST-TRAINING
HELPING ASSESSMENT**

**CHECKING OUT YOUR
COMMUNICATION SKILLS**

At the beginning of this book we got an index of your ability to communicate. Now let us get another index of your ability to communicate. You will be able to assess the progress you have made by comparing the results of this communication with the results of your earlier communication. When you formulate your responses, be sure that you at least make a response that captures the expressed feeling and meaning. If you can also provide direction, you will have made a complete response to the learner's expression. Please formulate in writing, then, the most helpful or effective responses which you might make to each of these learner expressions. Remember, write your response just as if you were talking to the learner. Each of the excerpts is presented by a different student so do not try to relate one excerpt to another. Learners presenting the expressions may be considered learners with whom you have come in contact in your daily living. Assume that you have interacted with them for an hour or more. They may or may not be formal learners. They may simply be kids who sought your help at a time of need.

FORMULATING HELPFUL COMMUNICATIONS

Please formulate your responses to the following learner expressions.

First Learner Expression:
"I didn't think I could do it, but now I'm doing the best in the whole class and now I know I can make it."

Your response: ⎯⎯⎯⎯⎯⎯⎯⎯⎯⎯

⎯⎯⎯⎯⎯⎯⎯⎯⎯⎯⎯⎯⎯⎯⎯⎯

⎯⎯⎯⎯⎯⎯⎯⎯⎯⎯⎯⎯⎯⎯⎯⎯

Second Learner Expression:
"I'm gonna get him back no matter what you do, I'm gonna get him back!"

Your response: ⎯⎯⎯⎯⎯⎯⎯⎯

⎯⎯⎯⎯⎯⎯⎯⎯⎯⎯⎯⎯⎯⎯⎯⎯

⎯⎯⎯⎯⎯⎯⎯⎯⎯⎯⎯⎯⎯⎯⎯⎯

Third Learner Expression:
"Sometimes I think I'm dumb!"

Your response: ⎯⎯⎯⎯⎯⎯⎯⎯

⎯⎯⎯⎯⎯⎯⎯⎯⎯⎯⎯⎯⎯⎯⎯⎯

Fourth Learner Expression:
"I'm really worried. If I don't make it this last marking period, my Dad is sure gonna get me good."

Your response: ⎯⎯⎯⎯⎯⎯⎯⎯

⎯⎯⎯⎯⎯⎯⎯⎯⎯⎯⎯⎯⎯⎯⎯⎯

⎯⎯⎯⎯⎯⎯⎯⎯⎯⎯⎯⎯⎯⎯⎯⎯

You should find that your communications are significantly more effective now than when you began this section due to a well-developed response repertoire.

CHECKING OUT YOUR
DISCRIMINATION SKILLS

Now let us take a final look at our ability to discriminate. Again, we will view the same four excerpts. In response to each of the student expressions, there are five alternative teacher responses. You should rate each of these responses on a scale from 1 to 5 as follows:

1—Very Ineffective
2—Ineffective
3—Minimally Effective
4—Very Effective
5—Extremely Effective

If you feel a response falls between two levels on a five-point scale, you may split the gap and rate 1.5, 2.5, 3.5 or 4.5.

First Learner Expression:
"I didn't think I could do it but now I'm doing the best in the whole class and now I know I can make it."

Please rate the following alternative teacher responses to the first excerpt.

_____1. *"That's nice."*
_____2. *"Now that you know that you have what it takes, you can start working even harder."*
_____3. *"You're feeling pretty happy about everything."*

_____4. *"You're really excited because you found out you have what it takes to do these things, and you really do want to succeed."*
_____5. *"It's exciting to become the best person you can be. It took a lot of work to follow through on your program and now you're getting ready for your next challenge. I'd like to help you develop your next program when you're ready."*

Second Learner Expression:
"I'm gonna get him back no matter what you do, I'm gonna get him back!"

Please rate the following alternative teacher responses to the second excerpt.

_____1. *"You're really angry with him because of what he's done to you."*
_____2. *"You're so angry with him you won't rest until you get him back. Let's talk about the advantages and disadvantages of some of the different ways of getting him back."*
_____3. *"You really ought to see if you can talk it over first before you do something that's gonna get you in trouble."*
_____4. *"You're so furious with him, that you know you won't feel the same inside until you do get him."*
_____5. *"Why don't you tell me what happened."*

DISCRIMINATING HELPFUL RESPONSES

Third Learner Expression:

"Sometimes I think I'm dumb!"

Please rate the following alternative teacher responses to excerpt three.

_____1. *"You feel sad because you're not doing well and you don't seem to be the person you'd really like to be. I think one of the things that we could do right now is to sit down and make up a way for you to study the things that get you down."*

_____2. *"Stop feeling sorry for yourself and get to work. We both know you can make it."*

_____3. *"You feel bad about your work."*

_____4. *"You're feeling pretty bad about your school work because it always seems to turn out poorly and you'd really like to do a lot better."*

_____5. *"We all feel that way some of the time."*

Fourth Learner Expression:

"I'm really worried. If I don't make it the last marking period, my Dad is gonna get me good."

Please rate the following alternative teacher responses:

_____1. *"You better get going."*

_____2. *"You feel scared because you're pretty sure it's not gonna turn out good."*

_____3. *"I don't think your Dad will do anything."*

_____4. *"You're frightened because you're always setting yourself up to lose. I think we're going to have to work out as careful a schedule for winning as you've already worked out for losing."*

_____5. *"You're scared because you are going to get it from your Dad and you really don't want that to happen."*

You should find that, due to a well-developed frame of reference, your discriminations are significantly more accurate than when you began interpersonal skills training.

OBTAINING YOUR DISCRIMINATION SCORE

In the table opposite are the ratings made by trained raters for each of the alternative teacher responses. Use this table to determine your discrimination score. First, find the difference between each of your ratings and the trained raters' ratings. Just look at the difference. It doesn't matter if the difference is positive or negative. Add all the different scores together and divide by 20. This is your discrimination score. You should find that your discrepancy scores are a half a level or less. This means that you do not disagree with the raters on whether the response is effective or ineffective. This means that you can accurately assess the progress you have made in communication.

Learner Expressions	Teacher Responses	Levels Responsiveness	Levels Initiative	Ratings	Your Ratings	Your Deviations
I	1	L	L	1.0	— =	
	2	L	H	2.0	— =	
	3	H	L	3.0	— =	
	4	H	H	4.0	— =	
	5	H	H+	5.0	— =	
II	1	H	L	3.0	— =	
	2	H	H+	5.0	— =	
	3	L	H	2.0	— =	
	4	H	H	4.0	— =	
	5	L	L	1.0	— =	
III	1	H	H+	5.0	— =	
	2	L	H	2.0	— =	
	3	H	L	3.0	— =	
	4	L	L	4.0	— =	
	5	H	H	1.0	— =	
IV	1	L	H	2.0	— =	
	2	H	L	3.0	— =	
	3	L	L	1.0	— =	
	4	H	H+	5.0	— =	
	5	H	H	4.0	— =	

Total = _____ = _____ = Discrimination Score

20

UNDERSTANDING WHERE YOU ARE
IN YOUR DISCRIMINATION SKILLS

Learning does not end with a post-training assessment of your discrimination level, even if it is a functional test that is related to your training experience. Even though your discrimination score improved significantly from the pre- to post-testing, you may have found that you had some difficulty rating some of the teacher responses. If we are to capture in its full richness the diversity of human communication, we must be able to deal in different feeling areas and with different learner concerns. In this regard, perhaps the level 5.0 responses are worth reviewing briefly. As can be seen in learner expression 1-teacher response 5, the learner is elated because where she is and where she wants to be converge for her. Still, she is preparing for the next challenge and the teacher takes the first step toward developing her program when she is ready. In learner expression 2-teacher response 2, the teacher takes the first step toward resolving the very difficult problem of needing to retaliate by involving the learner in a problem-solving process. In learner expression 3-teacher response 1, the teacher involves the learner in activities leading toward managing the school work that was getting her down. Finally, in learner expression 4-teacher response 4, the teacher begins to work out a program for *"winning"* with a learner who is fearful that she can no longer afford to be a *"loser."* All of these are difficult situations for us as teachers to address. And yet we must do so if we are to take the full human being into consideration. And we must do this if we are to teach effectively.

OBTAINING YOUR COMMUNICATION SCORE

Since you are now a trained rater yourself, you are qualified to assess your own levels of communication. First assign a rating to each of your two communication responses in the first part of this section. Compute your pre-training communication score by dividing the total of ratings by the number of responses which you made—two. In most cases, your pre-training communication score will fall between 1.0 and 2.0. This is where the vast majority of people from the teaching professions fall. If you rated yourself at 2.5 or above in the pre-test, be sure that you really have captured the feeling and meaning explicitly, as this would be an exceptionally high score for anyone to have who has not received prior communication training.

Now assign a rating to each of your post-training communication responses. Compute your post-training communication score by dividing by the total number of responses which you made, that is, four. You should find that you are receiving ratings at level 3.0 or above. Accordingly, you should find that you have improved a level or more in your interpersonal effectiveness. This will be primarily because you have learned to communicate your understanding of the learners.

Communication Level

Pre-Training

Learner Expression	Your Rating
I	_____
II	_____

Total = _____ = _____
      2   *Pre-Training Communication Level*

Post-Training

Learner Expression	Your Rating
I	_____
II	_____
III	_____
IV	_____

Total = _____ = _____
      4   *Post-Training Communication Level*

202

MASTERING INTERPERSONAL SKILLS

You know what there is to know about relating to the learners. You have more than the concept of communication. In relation to your learners, you know where you are and where you are going. You are going to help them to explore where they are so that they will be able to understand where they want to go. You know how to get them from where they are to where they want to go. Yes, you have more than the concept of communication. You have interpersonal skills.

You have the skills to control your class. To prevent the disturbances that prevent learning! To handle learning problems before they become discipline problems! You have the skills to increase the amount and quality of the basic skills you teach every day.

SUMMARY

UNDERSTANDING WHERE YOU ARE
IN YOUR TEACHING SKILLS

Let us summarize **where you are** in relation to your teaching skills. You are pleased with yourself because you have conquered communication skills. You acknowledge readily the critical nature of interpersonal skills: all learning begins with the learners' frames of reference. And you are happy because you now have the interpersonal skills to enter the learners' frames of reference. As a consequence of the communication training in this section, you have learned several interpersonal skills. In general, you have learned how to discriminate effective responses from ineffective responses. First, you have learned how to set the stage for teaching through attending, including attending physically, observing and listening. Second, you have learned to respond to where the learners are by responding interchangeably to the feelings and the reasons (meaning) for these feelings. Your

responsive skills enabled your learners to explore where they are. Third, you have learned to personalize your understanding of where your learners are and where they want to be. Fourth, you have learned to initiate programs that enable your learners to get from where they are to where they want to be. Now you can employ what you have learned in many different ways. You may link the interpersonal responses with whatever you have found to be effective in your teaching. For example, if you find asking questions, giving your opinion, or anything else appropriate, then do it—but follow it by responding to the learners' response to what you have initiated. Anything that you do that is meaningful will warrant a response. When a question does not elicit an answer that can be responded to by the teacher, it was a stupid question!

Teacher:	**Helping Skills**	Attending ▶	Responding	Personalizing	Initiating
Learners:	**Learning Skills**		Exploring	Understanding	Acting

WHERE YOU WANT TO BE
BECOMES WHERE YOU ARE

Where you want to be becomes **where you are** when you get there. Just as your pre-test gave you an index of where you were on your interpersonal skills, so your post-test now tells you whether you arrived where you wanted to be. If you worked effectively, you have indeed arrived. In a similar way, you may look at where you are in relation to your other teaching skills. Here again, your performance on the pre-tests will give you an index of where you are on your content-development and teaching delivery skills. On the other hand, you are eager to have a high level of expertise in these teaching skills. Your performance on the post-tests of teaching skills will define whether or not you reached where you wanted to be. Again, when you achieve a high level of functioning on the post-test, you will set your next objectives—perhaps in the area of career education or working skills. This movement can be seen most readily in program development where the subgoal of one program becomes the first step of the next program.

TEACHING YOUR LEARNERS
SELF-HELPING SKILLS

Now let us apply these principles to the learners whom you teach. The goal of the learners is to acquire something useful to them. The applications of learning in which they engage in class are unequal to useful skills in real-life activities. They may learn the skills you require of them to complete requirements. That is where they are. But they want to be able to transfer their skills into their real-life activities. That is where they want to be. How do you get them there from where they are to where they want to be? Easily! Just as you were trained in the skills to get you from where you were to where you wanted to be, so you can now teach your learners. You must ultimately teach the learners the skills which they require to get themselves—by themselves—from where they are to where they want to be.

TEACHING GETS YOU FROM WHERE YOU ARE TO WHERE YOU WANT TO BE IN YOUR TEACHING SKILLS

The answer to **how to get** anyone **from where they are** to **where they want to be** is always the same. Skills teaching! There is no other way to get there from here. Simply stated, you teach your learners what you learned. Just as you learned, so you now teach your learners: to attend; to respond; to understand; to initiate. Just as you learned interpersonal skills for teaching purposes, so you now teach your learners interpersonal skills for living purposes. There is no *"edge"* system here. Teaching is the preferred mode of helping anyone to get anywhere. It makes for a most honest and profound learning experience—for the teacher and the learner. Each lives and learns in order to live and teach what is worthwhile in life. It now remains for us to live and teach what is worthwhile in teaching skills. It remains for you to live and learn the teaching skills you need to know to get from where you are to where you want to be in your life. And to get your learners from where they are to where they want to be in their lives!

BIBLIOGRAPHY

Aspy, D.N.
Toward a Technology for Humanizing Education
Champaign, Illinois: Research Press, 1972
Useful for understanding the research base for the facilitative interpersonal dimensions of the Carkhuff Model in education. Contains introductions to Flanders Interaction Analysis and Bloom's cognitive processes as well as empathy, congruence and regard. Concludes that teachers with high levels of interpersonal skills have students who achieve more.

Aspy, D.N. and Roebuck, F.N.
Kids Don't Learn from People They Don't Like
Amherst, Massachusetts: Human Resource Development Press, 1977.
Useful for understanding the research base for the Carkhuff Model in teaching. Studies the differential effects of training in Flanders, Bloom and Carkhuff skills. Hundreds of teachers were trained. The effects on thousands of learners were studied. Significant gains were achieved on the following indices: student absenteeism and tardiness; student discipline and school crises; student learning skills and cognitive growth. Concludes that the Carkhuff model is the preferred teacher training model.

Berenson, B.G.
Belly-to-Belly and Back-to-Back: The Militant Humanism of Robert R. Carkhuff
Amherst, Massachusetts: Human Resource Development Press, 1975.
Useful for an understanding of the human assumptions underlying the human and educational resource development models of Carkhuff. Presents a collection of prose and poetry by Carkhuff. Concludes by challenging us to die growing.

Berenson, B.G. and Carkhuff, R.R.
The Sources of Gain in Counseling and Psychotherapy
New York: Holt, Rinehart and Winston, 1967.
Useful for an in-depth view of the different orientations to helping. Integrates the research of diverse approaches to helping. Concludes with a model of core conditions around which the different preferred modes of treatment make their own unique contributions to helpee benefits.

Berenson, B.G. and Mitchell, K.M.
Confrontation: For Better or Worse
Amherst, Massachusetts: Human Resource Development Press, 1974.
Useful for an in-depth view of confrontation and immediacy as well as the core interpersonal dimensions. Presents extensive experimental manipulation of core interpersonal skills and confrontation and immediacy. Concludes that while confrontation is never necessary and never sufficient, in the hands of an effective helper, it may be efficient for moving the helpee toward constructive gain or change.

Berenson, D.H., S.R. Berenson and Carkhuff, R.R.
The Skills of Teaching—Content Development Skills
Amherst, Massachusetts: Human Resource Development Press, in press, 1977.
Useful for learning skills needed for developing teaching content. Develops skills based content in terms of **do** and **think** steps and supportive knowledge in terms of facts, concepts and principles. Concludes that content must be developed programmatically in order to insure teaching delivery.

Berenson, S.R.; Carkhuff, R.R.; Berenson, D.H. and Pierce, R.M.
The Do's and Don'ts of Teaching
Amherst, Massachusetts: Human Resource Development Press, 1977.

Useful for pre-service and in-service teachers. Lays out the interpersonal skills of teaching and their effect in the most basic form. Concludes that effective teachers apply skills that facilitate their learners' involvement in learning.

Carkhuff, R.R.
Helping and Human Relations.
Vol. 1. Selection and Training
Vol. 2. Practice and Research
New York: Holt, Rinehart and Winston, 1969.

Useful for understanding the research base for interpersonal skills in counseling and education. Operationalizes the helping process in great detail. Presents extensive research evidence for systematic selection, training and treatment procedures. Concludes that teaching is the preferred mode of treatment for helping.

Carkhuff, R.R.
The Development of Human Resources:
Education, Psychology and Social Change
New York: Holt, Rinehart and Winston, 1971.

Useful for understanding applications of human resource development (HRD) models. Describes and presents research evidence for numerous applications in helping skills training in human, educational and community resource development. Concludes that systematic planning for human delivery systems can be effectively translated into human benefits.

Carkhuff, R.R.
The Art of Helping III
Amherst, Massachusetts: Human Resource Development Press, 3rd Edition, 1977

Useful for learning helping skills. Includes attending, responding, personalizing and initiating modules. Concludes that helping is a way of life.

Carkhuff, R.R. and Berenson, B.G.
Beyond Counseling and Therapy
New York: Holt, Rinehart and Winston, 2nd Edition, 1977.

Useful for understanding of the core interpersonal conditions and their implications and applications. Adds many core dimensions and factors them out as responsive and initiative dimensions. Includes an analysis of the client-centered, existential, psychoanalytic, trait-and-factor and behavioristic orientations to helping. Concludes that only the trait-and-factor and behavioristic positions make unique contributions to human benefits over and above the core conditions.

Carkhuff, R.R. and Berenson, B.G.
Teaching As Treatment
Amherst, Massachusetts: Human Resource Development Press, 1976.

Useful for understanding the development of a human technology. Operationalizes the helping process as teaching. Offers research evidence for living, learning and working skills development and physical, emotional and intellectual outcomes. Concludes that learning-to-learn is the fundamental model for living, learning and working.

Rogers, C.R.; Gendlin, E.T.; Kiesler, D.
and Truax, C.B.
**The Therapeutic Relationship and
Its Impact**
Madison, Wisconsin: University of
Wisconsin Press, 1967.

Useful for understanding the
transitional phases in developing
HRD models. Presents extensive
evidence on training lay and
professional helpers as well as different orientations to helping.
Concludes that the core interpersonal
dimensions of empathy, respect and
genuineness are critical to effective
helping.

Truax, C.B. and Carkhuff, R.R.
**Toward Effective Counseling
and Therapy**
Chicago, Illinois: Aldine, 1967.

Useful for understanding the
historical roots of the HRD models.
Presents extensive evidence on client-
centered counseling for schizophrenic
patients. Concludes that core interpersonal dimensions of empathy,
regard and congruence are critical to
effective helping.

Carkhuff, R.R.; Berenson, D.H. and
Berenson, S.R.
**The Skills of Teaching—
Lesson Planning Skills**
Amherst, Massachusetts: Human
Resource Development Press, in press,
1977.

Useful for learning skills needed to
prepare for delivering content.
Organizes lessons by reviewing,
overviewing, presenting, exercising
and summarizing. Breaks the
organization down into a tell-show-
do format. Concludes that content
must be delivered in programmatic
ways in order to maximize learning.

Carkhuff, R.R.; Devine, J.; Berenson, B.G.;
Griffin, A.H.; Angelone, R.; Keeling, T.;
Patch, W. and Steinberg, H.
Cry Twice!
Amherst, Massachusetts: Human
Resource Development Press, 1973.

Useful for understanding the
ingredients of institutional change.
Details the people, programs and
organizational variables needed to
transform an institution from a
custodial to a treatment orientation.
Concludes that institutional change
begins with people change.

Carkhuff, R.R and Pierce, R.M.
Teacher As Person
Washington, D.C.: National Education
Association, 1976.

Useful for teachers interested in
ameliorating the effects of sexism and
racism. Includes modules and applications of interpersonal skills in the
school. Concludes that behaviors
teachers practice influence learning
students accomplish.

NOTES

NOTES

NOTES

NOTES